Brilliant Passage

★ ★ ★

Brilliant Passage

. . . a schooning memoir

by Philip Gerard

Mystic Seaport Museum, Inc.
Mystic, Connecticut
1989

Designed by Marie-Louise Scull
Cover Photo: Ted Kelly, Photo-Boat
Printed and bound at The Nimrod Press, Boston

Table of Contents

for Kate

★ ★ ★

Sed mulier cupido quod dicit amanti,
In vento et rapida scribere oportet aqua.

—Catullus

Acknowledgments

For their parts in helping to make possible this voyage and this book, I owe debts of gratitude to the following people:

Sue Ellen Thompson and Stuart Parnes for giving me a home away from home in Mystic.

Captain George Moffett, for patiently answering all my questions and editing the original manuscript for accuracy, for help with research, for his good company, and for his expert seamanship.

Captain Francis E. "Biff" Bowker for allowing me to borrow details of *Brilliant*'s history and construction from his excellent article, "A Special Sort of Boat," *The Log of Mystic Seaport*, Summer 1982, and for critiquing the original manuscript for accuracy.

William W. Spivy and William M. Lauhaff, Jr., for their reminiscences about *Brilliant*'s wartime service.

Jerry Morris and Andy German of Mystic Seaport, who helped with research and whose editorial hands shaped these pages.

Alicia G. Crossman for making all the arrangements to get me aboard ship on short notice.

Lake Forest College for the summer grant-in-aid.

Ken, the baggage agent for Air Canada, Halifax, for recovering my duffel, lost by another airline, and sending it to me dockside by taxi at Air Canada's expense. And Air Canada for holding the Boston to Halifax flight and being so friendly about it all.

Our thanks to Mount Gay for their generous financial support following *Brilliant*'s winning of the 1986 American Schooner Association Series Trophy.

Doug Butler, Mate, for his good humor, companionship, and all that he taught me about seamanship.

Clint, Dean, Dave, Michelle, John, Liesel, and Mike—good shipmates all.

Walter Barnum, for the rare genius to know exactly what he wanted.

Sparkman & Stephens, who designed *Brilliant*, and all the crew of the Henry B. Nevins yard, who built her with such care and virtuosity.

Brilliant, for carrying us all safely over the wine-dark sea, home.

Lake Forest
October 29, 1987

Model of *Brilliant* built by Joe Appleton, ca. 1934.
(Photo by A.F. Sozio.)

1
★ ★ ★

Coming Aboard

There are only two stories worth telling, the late novelist John Gardner liked to say—A stranger comes to town, or someone goes on a journey. I came to Halifax a stranger to board the schooner *Brilliant* and go on a journey, a coastal passage that would take us into blue water: across the treacherous mouth of the Bay of Fundy, far offshore of Maine, Massachusetts, and Rhode Island, finally to a quiet berth on the Mystic River in Connecticut.

The voyage would not be extraordinary in rigor, hardship, or danger, might hardly qualify as a "voyage" to legendary blue-water skippers like Sir Francis Chichester and Philip Weld. But it would take us across the out-bound track of the fictional *Pequod* in quest of Moby Dick, across Herman Melville's own outbound track to the whaling grounds of the far Pacific; it would take us into the Gulf of Maine, home to one of the last great schooner fleets in the world; it would take us inshore of Georges Banks and the Grand Banks and through fleets of fishermen and lobstermen whose families have drawn their livelihoods from the sea for generations; it would take us to Nantucket Island, "the place where the first dead American whale was stranded," Melville says, launching at once a bloody nautical industry and the golden age of a nation's seapower; and it would take us to Vineyard Haven, Joshua Slocum's home port, from where, eleven restless years after his remarkable solo circumnavigation of the globe, he sailed forth one last time into a famous oblivion.

We would not be making history, but we certainly would be cruising waters over which the layers of history hung thick as the fog that settled on Halifax harbor every night. If on a chart of that parcel of the Atlantic you traced the voyages of every Norse longboat, Spanish galleon, Dutch caravel, Yankee clipper, every schooner, man-o'-war, frigate, pirate bark, fishing smack, trawler, dory, lobsterman, freighter, tanker, container ship, whaler, minesweeper, Liberty Ship, P.T. boat, destroyer, dreadnought, icebreaker, picket boat, submarine, sea-going tug, coastal packet, ocean liner, and yacht that had ever plied those waters, you would have a single broad black smear.

And the vessel that would take us through those waters was indeed extraordinary—a teak-hulled schooner yacht built in the depths of the Depression for the wealthy cousin of P.T. Barnum by some of the most skilled naval architects and boatbuilders in the world.

I came to *Brilliant* empty-handed, with just the clothes on my back and a notebook, feeling, I imagined, the way sailors the world over must feel when joining their ships in foreign ports—anxious to put water under them, eagerness tinged by apprehension for the adventure ahead. My blue duffel, into which I had carefully packed all my gear for the passage—camera, bed linens, towels, wool socks, a bulky fisherman's sweater, fingerless sailing gloves, rigging knife, wool hat, shore clothes, baseball cap, thermal underwear, rugby shirts, shorts, swim trunks, sea boots, toothbrush, razor, and storm gear—had missed the plane in Boston and would arrive by taxi only the night before our sailing.

Halifax on this early Saturday evening was overcast and already, two weeks into July, chilly. Water Street held the sheen of an intermittent drizzle. I passed behind the new high-rise hotels and followed an alley onto the quay, crowded with people in raucous good spirits. Not just boisterous teenagers, but couples young and old, mixed bands of boys and girls, ladies and gentlemen, promenading in a holiday sort of way. Saturday night in Halifax —folk music and the clink of glasses, the air bitten with brine and the aroma of steaming shellfish. I walked along the quay, past the replica of the *Bluenose*, probably the fastest and most famous fishing schooner ever built, past assorted small working craft and restaurants and the Canadian Bureau of Fisheries headquarters. Under yellow lamplight the waterfront looked clean as only a Canadian city's could be.

She was not hard to find—bow in, snugged to the Maritime Museum dock between two larger piers, over both of which rose high steel hulls and boxy, complicated superstructures. To starboard was C.S.S. *Acadia*, a decommissioned ocean research vessel, now in permanent berth at the museum. To port was H.M.C.S. *Sackville*, a camouflage-painted corvette of World War II vintage that had escorted lend-lease convoys across the Atlantic through the dread German U-boat patrols. Her gray anti-aircraft guns poked their harmless barrels skyward, breaking her squarish silhouette.

I had first laid eyes on *Brilliant* only a few weeks before, at Mystic, but I recognized the fair lines of her topsides immediately, the white spoon bow with the plain gold lettering of her name. She had the look that a vintage Martin guitar has, or a Steinway baby grand: a look that invited touching. To my disappointment, that time, I never went onboard. I stood on the dock and watched a maintenance crew polish and tidy and wash her down, and made up my mind then and there to sail on her.

She looked different somehow, now I knew I was going on board. As with another person, the prospect of intimacy with a sailing vessel holds both a certain thrill and the danger of disappointment.

Between those two unlovely obsolete ships, *Brilliant* rode perfectly still —hatches, skylights, and ports open to the dying breeze, mains'l and fores'l flaked neatly on their booms in a perfect harbor furl, rigging and lifelines shiny with wet.

In the cockpit, curled up on the lazarette cover beside the slanted helmsman's seat and writing in a spiral notebook, was Liesel, one of four teenage crew signed on for this trip. I called softly to her, and when she answered, I stepped aboard.

Later on I met Doug Butler, the mate, an amiable downeaster who, only twenty-seven, already had considerable experience as mate of the much larger Maine schooner *Adventure* and charter skipper of a Friendship sloop. Doug actually grew up in Hartford, Connecticut, but had spent eight years "downeast." He held a limited 100-ton certificate from the Coast Guard, allowing him to skipper a boat in coastal waters. Doug liked to hit the sack early, in port, given the scarcity of uninterrupted sleep offshore. Yet he never seemed less than alert in the dark hours of even the most strenuous graveyard watch. He had that quality I have come to notice in other men and women whose jobs entail a real physical responsibility for safety — pilots, long-haul truckers, cops — the sense of sustained total concentration on the job, for as long as it takes, replaced by an equally total relaxation once the job is finished.

Chilly in shirtsleeves and painter's pants, I still could not resist sitting up in the cockpit for awhile. I wrote what I saw in a black notebook, which would become my personal log:

Brilliant lies tethered on the glassy black water at the foot of a tall lighted city. Under the misted dock lights and the second-hand glow of the city, she gleams at her edges—bright varnish and brass against the flat smooth teak decks.

Wheel and binnacle are hooded in canvas the color of sand. At the center of the wheelcover is a small star. Understatement, a beauty mark. Overhead is the wooden mainboom, thick as a telephone pole, its outboard end nestled into the leather-padded pocket of the boom gallows aft of the cockpit, on the counter.

In front of me, the main companionway is dark. Brass-trimmed gauges set into the cabinhouse on either side of the opening all register zero or nothing at all—engine gauges to starboard, speedometer and depthsounder to port. Brass shines, shrouds are taut, lines are hung from belaying pins and booms in seamanlike fashion. The mainsheet, on the cabinhouse roof, is laid in a flemish coil. Brilliant is a lady used to being fussed over, used to the best.

Off our stern is moored Neith, a wooden Herreshoff cutter, also from Mystic. At either hand loom steel steamships—not modern, by any stretch. Above decks, with all their masts and rigging, they have the look of half-breeds, especially Acadia—of ships caught somehow in the evolutionary bind between wind and steam. It is an irony hardly worth stating that these "modern" ships are now just museum pieces, while Brilliant, a fifty-five-year-old wooden anachronism, sails on.

Straight off our bowsprit is the Maritime Museum, unlit. From its wharf rises a flag mast crossed by a spreader yard.

The mist is thick enough to wet these pages. The harbor fog signal sounds a low tone. Out of the fog comes ghosting a blue sailboat, mains'l flat, jib just barely drawing. Onboard a lone man is strumming a guitar, singing softly a verse and chorus of "The Boxer"—"I am just a poor boy though my story's seldom told . . . ." The boat drifts back into the fog.

People come and go along the wide dock and envy me, I imagine. I watch them look, see them wishing in their eyes. I feel privileged to be aboard, though I have not earned my passage, not yet. The water is glassy and black, almost oily. Occasional little swells—wakes?—cause the hull to rock like a big cradle.

3

Voices carry, as they will over water. Laughter, the earnest conversation of two kids, whispers. At intervals the Dartmouth ferry blasts its horn. The fog paints a nimbus around everything, making it slightly unreal, blotting equally the blue neon of the tall bank logo on the city's skyline and the channel lights at the ends of the piers. Definition is softened. Things blend. It's like looking at a scene and refusing to blink for so long that your eyes water.

Nothing is visible out in the harbor now—the fog is just too thick. I can still hear the faint thrumming of a wooden guitar across the water though, the muted tenor voice of the singer.

I go below.

Dave, a retired investment counselor who now had a select private practice, returned to the ship soon after. Dave had sailed on *Brilliant* often enough to know the routine and custom of shipboard life. He and Doug checked me out on the marine head aft, just forward of the navigator's station. The crucial point, Doug explained, was to close the sea-cock after flushing, or else risk flooding the whole cabin. Then Dave steered me to a port side quarter berth from where I could smell the ocean and feel the refreshing harbor-damp breeze as I lay stripped under clean wool blankets, winding down from the physical and psychological fatigue of modern travel (Chicago to Boston by jet, a mad sprint across three terminals to the waiting Air Canada flight to Halifax, polite customs interview and lost baggage forms to fill out and a slow bus into the city proper), and rocking to a gentle sleep to the rhythm of the foghorn.

My body, at least, balks at being carried too far too fast. My mind heats up like an overloaded engine after too many hours of dealing with strangers, paperwork, questions and answers, the documents of travel. It all happens too fast. The sudden stomach-clenching rush of takeoff and landing, and in between the blur of high altitude climate-controlled boredom. Tense closed-up strapped-in tight boredom.

There in my bunk (the chart table, as it turned out) I was beginning to fall into a different rhythm—an old-fashioned, slower rhythm, not of supersonic speed and video screens and heavy traffic, but of a deep-throated foghorn and the musical creak of rigging and the soft voices of lovers strolling the dock, their own private romances made more real by the romance of this wooden ship before them in the glaze of misty light.

Tomorrow I would renew my acquaintance with George Moffett, Captain of the *Brilliant*, whom I had been introduced to in Mystic, and I would meet the rest of the crew: Clint and Dean, artisans from the Mystic Seaport Museum serving respectively as ship's cook and deckhand; the other teens: Michelle, daughter of a Coast Guard officer and seasoned small-boat sailor; John, tall and fit, a football player who always seemed to be on hand when any strenuous task was called for; and Mike, last to arrive, more reserved than the others at first, but equally at home on deck.

4

Brilliant becalmed at the start of the 1933 Fastnet Race. (Photo courtesy Beken of Cowes, Ltd.)

We had a whole day left to prepare for sea. For now I lay and listened. There is nothing like sleeping on a sailboat, no bed quite so restful. I had slept often on my little cutter up on Roosevelt Lake, in faraway desert Arizona, and never felt so safe as with water under me. We had a whole day left of polishing, loading, stowing, safety and seamanship drill, and leave-taking, before we cast off lines and got underway. But I was snug aboard, and insofar as any voyage takes place partly in the imagination, for me this one had already begun.

2

★ ★ ★

Maritime Museum Dock
Halifax, N.S.

From my log:

The shipboard day begins early. When we hear the mate stirring, we roll out of our bunks, then fold and stow our bedding in the two lockers midships. The first order of business on Brilliant *is to wipe down all the brightwork (varnished wood) with chamois cloths: cockpit coamings, cabinhouse, helmsman's seat, lazarette hatches, mooring bits, skylights, bulwarks. This is done to dry them of dew and preserve the varnish. Like many chores aboard* Brilliant, *it is also done for appearances.* Brilliant *is, after all, a sail-training vessel, the traveling showpiece of Mystic Seaport Museum, and she must at all times look shipshape. This is not vanity but pride.*

Next comes the brass polishing. Daily, at least at mooring and when sailing in fair weather, the exterior brass must be buffed to a high shine—all seventeen winches and handles, the large hexagonal binnacle, the wheel hub, mooring bit-heads, gauges, bulwarks, footplates. In the course of a single season, all that brass gear will absorb two dozen cans of polish—literally gallons of the stuff.

The captain himself takes the lead in these chores, which surprises and pleases me. Here is a captain who leads by example—a harder method than pulling rank. The whole crew is responsible for maintenance, and after the first day we all wipe and polish without being told. We get used to the gray film under our fingernails, We watch where we put our hands, careful not to sully a shipmate's handiwork.

By now it is eight o'clock—0800 hours, eight bells—and time for flags. The Stars & Stripes is fastened to the jackstaff at the stern, while the red "Brilliant" and blue "Mystic Seaport" pennants are run up the main and foremasts, respectively. Once underway, the expensive pennants will be hauled down and replaced by a nylon wind sock to keep them from becoming tattered.

Halifax is already warming up. The harbor fog is thinning, burning off. We speculate out loud about how thick it will be offshore. Over breakfast at the Bluenose Cafe, Captain Moffett goes over final provisioning plans with Doug, Clint, and Dean. Groceries, ice, and Sterno must still be loaded. The ice, at least, will wait until tomorrow.

The day passes slowly, feeling like Sunday—a couple of hours at the towboat dock and wandering through the Maritime Museum with George, admiring models of windjammers and supertankers, of our dockside neighbors Acadia *and* Sackville; *the collection of lifesaving equipment, including a Lyle gun for shooting line to a vessel in distress and a fully preserved double-ended surfboat on its carriage; and the fleet of small classic yachts, all sail flying indoors, premier among them an original bluenose sloop, cocky and tall, a slippery hull depending on a deep fin keel to counterbalance her high rig.*

Late in the day, now that all the crew have reported aboard, the skipper and mate conduct safety and seamanship drills.

From a below-decks locker handy to the companionway, George draws a lifejacket and demonstrates the proper way to lace it on and activate the attached miniature flashing beacon. He explains how to launch the man-overboard pole mounted to the port lifelines—just tug on the ring and it drops clear, attached to a yellow horseshoe buoy with floating line, its flashing beacon automatically activated to help locate the victim. "I don't have to tell you," he says, "that if you go overboard at night or in the fog the chances of our finding you are pretty slim." We nod, and think about that.

Some years back, in Fisher's Island Sound, a Girl Scout crew member fell overboard from *Brilliant*'s bow pulpit. Captain Francis E. "Biff" Bowker, then master of the *Brilliant*, never saw her go over. "As we sailed by her I heard this little voice," he says, "and there she was in the water." Captain Bowker immediately took over the helm and ordered his Girl Scout crew to keep an eye on the girl in the water. "But instead they all went below and got their cameras," he remembers. "Luckily, it was a calm sea and we had no trouble circling back to pick her up." Headsails were struck and the engine started and within minutes the girl climbed back aboard using the swim ladder.

On another occasion, again off Fisher's Island, a teenage deckhand had his hat blown off by gusty winds; when he stood up to grab for it, he himself was blown clear across the cabinhouse to the lee rail, where he caught up against the lifelines.

But the danger of going overboard really doesn't register yet, not with the sun shining and the Sunday crowd on the dock eavesdropping on this curious lecture about calamity. George's manner is matter-of-fact. He is not a man who overreacts. His tone is calm but full of authority, and we all listen intently.

On the port side, handy to the cockpit, hangs a second yellow horseshoe buoy. Ordinarily, Brilliant carries the more traditional white O-rings mounted at the stern on the boom gallows. The new yellow buoys are a precaution for the offshore work she will do this trip.

Next, George takes us forward of the cabinhouse and points out two canvas-covered drums. He strips the cover off one, revealing a white two-piece canister that resembles a small cartop carrier. These are the 6-person Givens inflatable life rafts, designed with canopies against exposure to the elements and ballast bags to keep them upright in steep breaking seas, and for use only if the ship should be in imminent danger of sinking. One is for the captain's watch, the other for the mate's. The drill is for two crewmen to unfasten the drum, free its coil of line to run, toss the drum overboard, then yank the line, which will cause the raft to inflate from a CO_2 cylinder, and finally cut it loose from the ship. "If it doesn't inflate on the first try, yank it again," George says. "Load on the freshwater containers, then step into the raft as carefully as you can, and try not to get wet."

Again we all nod, as if we have been through this before.

He looks at all of us and then, like the boarding school headmaster he used to be, asks each of us to repeat the steps of the procedure.

A few minutes later we gather in the cockpit around the captain and his two "grabbags," red nylon duffels, again one for each watch. He fishes out each item and explains its use: first-aid kit, backup to the ones on the rafts; knife with a dulled point (so as not to puncture the air chambers of the life-raft); gaff for fishing; sunburn lotion; hand-held flares and rocket flares; spare line; and a softcover book of rescue stories. "So you'll be able to read about just how bad it's going to get before you're rescued," George says, a hint of irony in his voice. His sense of humor is flat, almost British in its subtlety.

We laugh, nervously.

I watch and listen, but it still seems absurd to imagine Brilliant *being overwhelmed by seas or wind.*

Walter Barnum (left) and Joe Appleton, who frequently sailed aboard *Brilliant*, admire Appleton's model of her, ca. 1934. (Photo by A.F. Sozio.)

8

Captain George told of *Brilliant*'s having weathered, more than once, a steady 40-knot blow on the nose. "And she can run safely in forty knots," he maintained. "That would not bother me. She's built for that." Even a rogue gust of 80 knots, which hit *Brilliant* in New York harbor some years back with George at the helm, could knock her down only to 65 degrees of heel. "And she has to go all way down to seventy-six degrees," he said, "before she starts downflooding through the aft Dorade vents."

When Walter Barnum (1887–1966) commissioned his schooner, as yet unnamed, from the prestigious naval architecture firm of Sparkman and Stephens, he did so in no uncertain terms. He was, after all, president of the Pacific Coast Company, a wealthy capitalist of railroads, coal mines, cement plants, and lumber mills. Barnum was a seasoned deep-water sailor besides, and not a man to cut corners.

The schooner was to be a present from his wife—she actually paid for the boat.

In a letter to Drake H. Sparkman in 1930, after his initial meeting with the firm and before *Brilliant* had even got to the drawing board stage, Barnum was explicit: "I believe you also understand that while the ship may never go around the world, she is to be designed as though that end were definitely in view. I feel we should always keep before us a mental picture of her hove to in the middle of the North Atlantic, with the wind at eighty miles an hour and seas in proportion."

He reminded them of an adventure survived by the *Cutty Sark* in the Roaring Forties—the great ship was swamped by seas so mountainous that, to the terrified sailors clinging to the yards aloft, her hull and deck were completely invisible underwater for minutes at a time. He wanted that kind of survivability built into a private yacht.

Barnum went even further. He followed up the letter with his detailed "Specifications for Schooner." He expected his new boat, he wrote, to be . . .

1. *Capable of being rolled over in a hurricane and coming up again with hull, and deck opening covers intact.*
2. *To lie steadily in a full gale and in a heavy sea.*
3. *To have a rudder and steering gear as nearly unbreakable as possible including some kind of friction or spring gear at rudder head to take jars of sea when hove to. Something perhaps that can be thrown in or out of gear. Suggest something similar to Electric Locomotive Driving Gear. [In fact, Brilliant's steering relies on a simple overbuilt worm gear connecting rudderhead to wheel shaft—which has never needed repair.]*
4. *To have lower masts stepped and stayed to stand any conceivable strain that might be placed upon them short only perhaps [perhaps!] of a complete capsizing. [Estimated breaking strain of one side of the main rigging: 78 tons.]*
5. *To be as heavily timbered, planked and decked as is reasonably possible, eliminating at the same time any really unnecessary weight where maximum strength or at least ample strength to meet first specification can be secured by closeness and quality of timbering, fastening, bracing, etc., etc.*
6. *Quality and number of fastenings to be maximum consistent with good practice.*

7. *Nothing left undone to eliminate the possibility of rot anywhere.*
8. *Ventilation of bilges, lockers., etc., to be given full study to obtain best and most certain possible system using natural rather than mechanical circulation. [Hence, the six large skylights and four Dorade vents.]*
9. *Every piece of material, whether wood or metal, to be literally perfect for the use intended.* [Brilliant's builders used only non-ferrous metals, for instance—bronze and monel, an alloy of nickel, copper, manganese, silicon, and carbon—both highly corrosion-resistant.]

Here was a yachtsman demanding *literal perfection* in a boat intended to be as nearly indestructible as shipwrights could make her. But lest Sparkman and Stephens balk at the prospect of building a floating tank, Barnum insisted also on performance:

10. *To be as fast and weatherly as possible, consistent with all of above.*
11. *To be as handsome as possible consistent with all of above.*
12. *Hull and rig design to be in no way adversely affected by any accommodation requirements.*

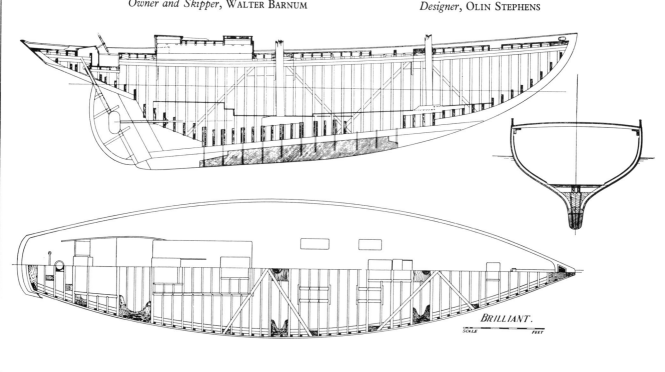

BRILLIANT

Length, overall	- - -	61 ft. 6 in.	Length, water-line -	- 49 ft. 0 in.
Beam	- - - -	14 ft. 8 in.	Draught - - -	- 8 ft. 10 in.
Displacement	- - -	38¼ tons	Sail area - -	- 2,082 sq. ft.

Owner and Skipper, WALTER BARNUM   *Designer,* OLIN STEPHENS

Brilliant's hull under
construction at the Nevins
yard, 16 October 1931.
(Rosenfeld Collection,
Mystic Seaport Museum.)

On the face of it, Barnum was demanding the impossible, a perfect compromise between speed and beauty on the one hand and seaworthiness and durability on the other—an exaggeration of the perennial dilemma faced by all cruising yacht builders. For *Brilliant* was indeed designed for fast cruising, not for racing, as Barnum made clear in a 1963 letter to Francis E. "Biff" Bowker, master of the *Brilliant* for over twenty years: "I was most specific in planning *Brilliant* to get the idea across to her designer that she was not to be designed or built for racing. In order to nail it down, I told Olin [Stephens] flatly that I would probably never race her."

But instead of a floating tank, what brothers Rod and Olin Stephens and the Henry B. Nevins Yard of City Island, New York, produced was a masterpiece of fair lines, clean deck layout, and comfortable belowdecks, that could stand up to extraordinary conditions and, coincidentally, race with the greyhounds.

She competed in the 1932 Bermuda Race almost immediately after her 23 April launching, blew out her genoa the first night offshore, but finished close behind *Highland Light*'s new course record and rated fouth on corrected time.

The following year she ran from Nantucket Lightship to Bishop Rock Light, England, in 15 days, 1 hour, and 23 minutes—a record for a vessel of her size. That passage, on which she logged 215 miles a day at an average speed of over nine knots, is commemorated on a brass plaque affixed to the overhead beam immediately as you enter the companionway, along with two framed photographs of *Brilliant* then and now.

She had run her latest race, Marblehead to Halifax, with a teenage crew. Light airs had sabotaged her chances, though. To show her stuff, *Brilliant* needs a stiff breeze. Big wind. As Captain George points out, "*Brilliant* has shown her stuff as a classic among other classics in recent traditional boat regattas."

Belowdecks, the sturdiness of *Brilliant*'s construction and the care of her workmanship were apparent to me from the first. Her 1 7/8-inch teak planks over oak frames, wrote Captain Bowker in an article for *The Log of Mystic Seaport*, were "so well shaped, fastened, and caulked, that it was not until 1978 that it became obvious that some of the seams should be recaulked." That sort of report inspires confidence in an offshore hull, as does the fact (also pointed out by Bowker) that *Brilliant*'s 1 3/8-inch bronze keel bolts did not require tightening until 1979.

BUILT BY NEVINS . . .

WALTER BARNUM

Dartmouth, Devon.
July 9th, 1933.

Dear Mr. Nevins:

You can be just as proud of "Brilliant" as you like. She has gone and made all kinds of records in spite of her aged crew, who started out determined to make a leisurely cruise and ended up by breaking almost all the records in sight as far as I know and as far as my experienced and well informed crew knows. We sailed her through two gulf stream squalls, both of which Al Loomis estimated at 60 miles, with all plain sail — like a dude. She has never parted or started anything alow or aloft. She made a record run across and leaked not a drop through deck or hull. The big ventilators have never been off and no water came in the skylights. I pumped her once, to get rid of some kerosene we spilled in the bilge (our only accident) or rather, I was able to pump her only after pumping a ton of water into her to sweeten her up. There wasn't enough to start the pump before.

We sailed 1087 miles in 5 days, 1449 in a week, and 1945 in ten days.

There you have the highlights. All hands agreed they had never been in such a dry ship. Our shore clothes and shoes looked as though they had come from the tailor — no dampness or mildew. It's all most satisfactory. We had no heavy following breezes. She simply never stops. It takes very little to make her go eight knots and not much more to do nine. Olin Stephens has certainly given her miraculous lines for such a heavy boat.

Please tell all the boys they certainly turned out the best ever. She sits in Dartmouth Harbor as spic and span as ever.

Sincerely yours,

(Signed) WALTER BARNUM.

BRILLIANT
Designed by Sparkman & Stephens

> *"Mr. Walter Barnum's gaff-rigged schooner . . . She is all solid teak, and I never saw a finer and more honest piece of boatbuilding and rigging in my life."*
>
> *Weston Martyr*
> *Yachting World — London*

JOHN R. HOGAN
ARCHITECTS BUILDING
PHILADELPHIA

Henry B. Nevins, Inc.,
City Island, N. Y.

July 13, 1932.

My dear Mr. Nevins:

Now that the AYESHA has been tested in a hard driving race under more severe conditions than she was designed for, I want to tell you that I am very much pleased with the way in which you built her.

To finish third in her class in the Bermuda Race with no chance to tune her up in advance meant hard punishment to the boat, which she took without a creak or a strain, without leaking, and without anything carrying away, more than justifying our confidence in her design and construction. The paint and varnish held up remarkably well and there is practically nothing to show that she has been through the hardest kind of service.

I am also pleased with the efficiency and courtesy of you and your organization, with whom it has been a real pleasure to work, and who furnished unending surprise that you could accomplish so much in so short a time.

AYESHA
Designed by Philip Rhodes

The beauty and excellence of the workmanship has been remarked by all who have been aboard, and I do not believe a better boat could be built anywhere in this country or abroad.

Sincerely,

(Signed) JOHN R. HOGAN.

It's real economy to deal with Nevins because they know "what to do and how to do it"

HENRY B. NEVINS, INC.
CITY ISLAND, NEW YORK CITY

A competent designing staff headed by George F. Crouch is at the service of individuals for designs, or for the carrying out of designs of any naval architect

Brilliant cost a total of $100,000: $15,000 to design, $85,000 in labor and materials to build. A proper price tag would have been closer to $160,000. The Nevins yard made little, if any, profit.

In 1963, when Barnum visited the old schooner for the first time in many years, he felt right at home. He wrote of that visit, "I was equally thrilled to find everything on deck precisely as it had always been with every cleat, winch, pad eye, and sheet lead so familiar that I felt I had been born with it. It was a very great thing for me."

Except for a change in her mainsail, *Brilliant* looked the same when I met her as she had the day she was launched some fifty-five years before: sixty-one feet, six inches in length overall, forty-nine feet in length at the waterline, with a beam of fourteen feet eight inches and a draft of eight feet ten inches. She still carried 33,000 pounds of lead in her keel, displaced 84,420 pounds (42 tons), and registered 30 tons, gross.

Brilliant hauled at Mystic Seaport's shipyard to be recaulked for the first time since her launch, 1979. (Photo by Kenneth E. Mahler)

opposite

Barnum's tribute to the Nevins yard for the construction of *Brilliant* appeared in the September 1933 issue of YACHTING.

15

Walter Barnum (left)
reminisces with mate Dick
DeWick, Robert Damm, and
Captain Francis E. Bowker at
Mystic Seaport, June 1963.
(Seaport Photo Archives)

I wasn't worried about capsize or sinking. *Brilliant* had been built to rise
to the motion of the water, and she had been built well.

The final exercise in the drill was to buckle on safety harnesses and
make our way, one at a time, out to the stainless-steel pulpit on the end of
the bowsprit. The nylon tether of the harness was carabinered onto one of
two quarter-inch deck jacklines running the length of the deck. Always go
forward on the weather side, Doug advised us. Then, at the bow, unsnap

16

from the cable and hook onto the cable that runs along the bowsprit, again on the weather side. Get a firm hold on the handrails and step carefully along the footropes, leaning perpendicularly against the bowsprit.

"Make sure of each handhold before you take the next step," Doug said. "The Gloucester fishermen used to call this thing the 'widowmaker.'"

The kids went first, all of them agile, then it was my turn. I buckled in, then made my way out to the pulpit at the end of the eleven-foot-long bowsprit stiffly, a little timidly. While the Sunday dockside crowd looked on, I gripped the handrails and climbed along the footropes, here in the gentle harbor swells practicing against the time, very soon now, when I would have to do it out on the ocean in less ideal conditions.

There was more drill to come.

Doug directed us to the running backstays, where we took turns seating the tensioning line on the winch. "Three turns, then haul it back to the cleat," he said. "Make sure you have a good lead. Put on a couple of figure-eights, no half-hitch." The handier to free it when tacking, or jibing.

We teamed up by turns winching down the main halyard, then practiced coiling finger-thick dacron jib and fisherman stays'l sheets until we could all do them fast and neat.

George spread out charts in the sunny cockpit and we gathered around. Tomorrow morning, after the fog lifted from the harbor, we would get underway for the first leg of our sail, some 340 miles to Nantucket. But, he went on, if the fog was still with us by the time we reached Nantucket Sound, we might change our itinerary: too many playful whales and dangerous shoals out there to come up on them without a reliable lookout.

Before supper, our first onboard meal, the crew was invited for a last hot shower on the *Acadia*. There would not be time before putting to sea in the morning. My duffel arrived in timely fashion, and I went up the gangway of *Acadia* and down into her crew's shower room to finally wash the travel off me and put on fresh clothes. For supper, all ten of us crowded into the main saloon around the ingenious folding table and gimballed serving tray hung on the mast above it. It would be our last meal as a whole crew for the duration.

From now on, we would eat in watches: Captain George, Dave, Michelle, John, and Clint on the A-watch; Doug, Dean, Liesel, Mike, and I on the B-watch.

The watches would alternate according to the so-called Swedish system: 8 A.M. to 1 P.M.; 1 P.M. to 7 P.M; 7 P.M. to 12 midnight; midnight to 4 A.M.; 4 A.M. to 8 A.M. (or, if you like, 0800 to 1300; 1300 to 1900; 1900 to 2400; 2400 to 0400; 0400 to 0800). This arrangement would insure that no one watch would have to stay up all night long, when cold and fatigue would be most likely and alertness and concentration most valuable.

But the real virtue of this system was that the A and B watches would alternate days on the long midday rest (1–7 P.M.). As a rule, this watch system is most valuable on really long passages. Captain George used it in honor of Waldo Howland, who described it in his book, *A Life in Boats*, a copy of which was shelved in the main saloon.

17

In the evening a contingent of local mariners paid us a courtesy call: Peter, a harbor pilot; a towboat (tugboat, in U.S. usage) skipper named Bill whose wheelhouse we had visited earlier that afternoon; Ed Murphy, master and owner of the *Hebride*; and his daughter Annette. We filled up the main saloon, its Honduras mahogany paneling burnished by the glow of a ship's lantern. We adults sipped Johnny Walker scotch, "Redjacket," courtesy of our captain. (Before casting off next day, George locked away all the booze; there would be no alcohol consumed on board while underway.)

Bill, a ringer for the late actor Robert Shaw both in physical appearance and manner of speech, warmed to the scotch and the company and told long and hilarious stories of his seagoing exploits, culminating in an outlandish yarn about the time he caught a monstrous 400-pound rubber-backed turtle while trolling for swordfish and how he chained the poor creature to the deck in a heroic and vain attempt to deliver it to a research aquarium. His crew at last threatened mutiny, and he reluctantly hoisted the snapping turtle with a tackle and dumped it over the side.

Captain Murphy teased the harbor pilot, Peter, and Peter teased back with tales of all sorts of maritime misadventures in which the culprit was always, naturally, a schooner. A windbag.

I asked Murphy why he owned a schooner. "You need such a big crew just to sail her," I said. "Then there's all the maintenance of a big wooden ship, all the expense."

He looked at me in a kind of mild surprise, as if he'd never considered the question before. "What else would I have?" he said. "I wanted a *real* boat." Everybody nodded over his cup, even the pilot, as if they all knew exactly what he meant. I suppose they did. "Tradition," Captain Murphy said. "I guess it's a kind of tradition."

After the guests had gone back to their boats, I found myself sitting in the cockpit with Clint. Clint looked exactly the way you'd expect a windjammer sailor to look—not large-framed, but strong and wiry and agile; longish blond hair and full blond beard; brick-tanned the way only a fair-skinned man could be; in his teeth a pipe, always, no matter what the weather or what his hands were doing (I have photos of Clint on bow lookout, Clint overhauling a line, Clint grinding the mains'l halyard winch, always with a lit pipe in his mouth). There was something rakish about him.

In real life, he was the Mystic Seaport Museum blacksmith, with the inflated forearms to prove it. On his left arm, just below the elbow, was tattooed a lightning bolt. He spoke with an accent—not exactly British, not exactly anything you could place as American. He declined, smiling, to say where he was from, but he'd tell you where he'd been—Britain, New York, Maine, Canada, the Caribbean.

Clint was a little sorry to be leaving Halifax. The people here, he said, had been good to him. I understood what he meant. In only the short time I had spent there, I had realized that Halifax was a city that understood ships and mariners, especially wind ships and sailors. The waterfront was distinct but still a part of the city proper, and of the city's business—not an isolated slum. There are precious few cities like that left.

18

Clint had his eye on a lifeboat that had been discarded at a junkyard back in Mystic, he confided. He wanted to buy it and rig it for sail. Maybe add a cabin, the way the eccentric Davies had done in *The Riddle of the Sands*. And what vessel could be more seaworthy than a lifeboat? He sat with me and smoked and dreamed out loud about the boat he would make his own.

"Sailboats make sense to me," Clint said, blowing out smoke. "The wind comes from somewhere, you work your sails, and the boat goes somewhere, you know?"

With that he went ashore for one last walk around the quiet city.

3
★ ★ ★

Pennant Point
to Brazil Rock

We woke to harbor traffic in the heavy fog—so heavy it was more like a drizzle. Construction gangs on the high-rise skeletons behind the waterfront were already hammering and riveting and slamming steel girders into place. The busy port was back to work after a leisurely weekend, and it was time for us to go.

We unfurled the Stars & Stripes, then ran up a Canadian flag on the starboard spreader of the foremast (it is customary, in foreign waters, to fly as a "courtesy ensign" the flag of the host country). We raised the red "Brilliant" burgee, white capital letters on a red swallowtail background, on the mainmast flag halyard, affixing it staff and all with two clove hitches, then got up the "Mystic" pennant, a blue capital M inside a white diamond on a blue field, in the same fashion on the foremast.

Clint confided to me after setting flags that he expected a hard wet sail and plenty of dirty weather between here and the Mystic River. Watching the fog, it was hard to disagree. This was the thickest I had seen it in three days, and a light but steady breeze was blowing out of the southwest—from exactly the direction we needed to go after clearing harbor. That would make for a bumpy ride.

But for the time being, there were ice blocks to load and last-minute chores to be done. We breakfasted in two shifts on flapjacks, orange juice, and plenty of strong aromatic coffee. On board ship, good coffee is the key to a successful galley.

Doug and Michelle pulled up dockside in a taxi and began offloading sacks of groceries—cold cuts by the pound, bread, fruit, peanut butter, jelly, juices, soft drinks, canned vegetables, cookies. Then they handed aboard three canvas tote bags, each containing a fifty-pound block of ice. We formed a kind of bucket brigade to get the stuff off the dock quickly and down through the midships scuttle into the capacious iceboxes in the galley.

The midships scuttle offered direct access to the galley down a vertical ladder. Moreover, even in bad weather, it was a good place for the cook and his "galley slave" (determined by a loose rotation) to get some fresh air, as it was sheltered on three sides by glass and wood and hooded with a canvas spray dodger; it could be closed tightly by sliding in boards across the opening aft. Often during the passage I saw Clint's ruddy face, pipe clenched in his mouth, framed in the scuttle opening. There, protected from wind and spray, he smoked to his heart's content and kept an eye on the deck watch.

Brilliant was a survivor of the era of professional yachting, when wealthy owners stayed aft with their guests—usually in rather posh accommodations —and the paid crew kept to the forecastle (pronounced "fo'c'sle," named for the "castle" erected on the foredeck of ancient sailing vessels to house crews and soldiers). Traditionally, professional yacht crews went uniformed. Often, they went barefoot as well.

"On sailing vessels where going aloft was necessary, bare feet would be safer than shoes, which might fall off," Captain George explained. "If your feet are accustomed to being bare aloft, it is very good for sure footing in warm weather." But he himself preferred a shod crew. Even on *Brilliant*'s clean deck there were too many cleats, blocks, and hard gear to cut and bruise bare toes.

Joiner work in the saloon. The engine room and chain drive linkage are visible forward. (Rosenfeld Collection, Mystic Seaport Museum.)

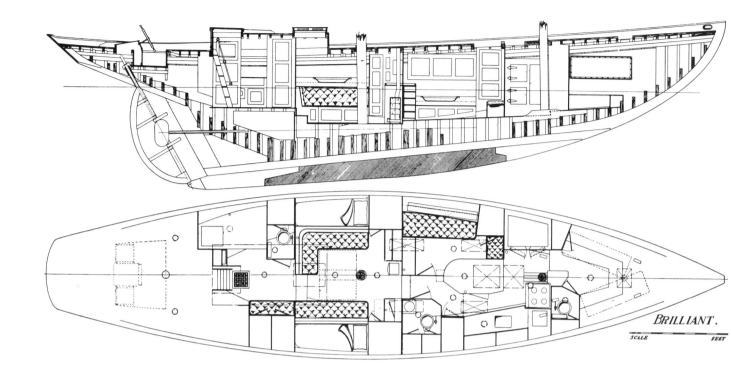

BRILLIANT.

SCALE   FEET

Saloon, looking forward,
1932. (Rosenfeld Collection,
Mystic Seaport Museum.)

opposite, top left
Stateroom, 1932.
(Rosenfeld Collection,
Mystic Seaport Museum.)

opposite, top right
Midship head, one of three,
1932. (Rosenfeld Collection,
Mystic Seaport Museum.)

opposite, bottom
Galley, 1932.
(Rosenfeld Collection,
Mystic Seaport Museum.)

Brilliant's fo'c'sle, with its four bunks stacked symmetrically into the V formed by the bow, its own cramped head, and its own hatch opening on the foredeck, had already been appropriated by the teens (or "kids," as they called themselves).

On *Brilliant*, in between the spacious main saloon, with its two stacked sea-berths and two more settee bunks, and the fo'c'sle, were, in order, the captain's cabin, the engine room, the midships head, and the galley. The captain's cabin, formerly the owner's stateroom, contained bunkbeds for the captain (lower) and the mate (upper), as well as dresser and mirror and, covering the wall separating it from the engine room, a panel of dials, gauges, and switches that monitored the engine and controlled recharging of ship's batteries.

We handed down the last bag of ice, which George and Clint squared away behind the thick wooden doors of the icebox.

The crew stood by bow line, stern line, and spring lines on deck while the captain held a final conference with Jeff Stone, the skipper of *Neith*, who, only months before, had been George's mate on *Brilliant*. They talked about the weather, and most of the news was bad. There was a big low out there, and fog along an extensive front offshore. Jeff's original plan, assuming the fog was only local, had been to follow *Brilliant* out of the crowded harbor into open water, as *Brilliant* was fitted with radar and *Neith* was not. But with fog this thick and no prospect of it lifting for days, Jeff opted to stay in port, wait out the fog, then coast-hop home, sailing only in daylight.

They shook hands and George stepped aboard. He fired up the diesel engine and listened to it throb for a few minutes, then, satisfied, gave the order to cast off all lines. Dean and Clint, on the dock, slipped the lines off the pilings and we hauled them quickly on deck as the two jumped aboard. George put the wheel over and levered the engine into reverse, then backed us out of our slip as neatly as if he were backing a compact car out of a parking space.

On the dock, some museum employees had gathered, along with a scattering of tourists, to see us off. They waved. We waved back. George handled the wheel casually, standing, put the engine in neutral, and our stern drifted around until we were pointed to the harbor mouth. Dean scurried out along the bowsprit to the pulpit, George engaged the engine, and, at 0935 hours on 13 July, we were underway.

"A" watch was on duty, so I could relax and enjoy our leave-taking. Dave took the wheel and George ducked down the companionway to check his charts. The bunk I had used for two nights in port was now off-limits, as it had become the chart-table. On the bulkhead over the bunk, just inside the companionway and protected by a wood and glass spray screen, were mounted the electronic aids to navigation: Horizon VHF radio and Stevens Engineering Associates SSB radio model 223, for local and long-distance communications with shore stations and other vessels*; Raytheon Raynav 750 Loran-C for plotting position; Data Marine depth finder and speedo, whose digital read-outs were displayed in the cockpit; and Raytheon 1200 Mariners Pathfinder Radar, for keeping clear of other vessels and hazards to navigation, and supplementing course information.

Under the chart table/bunk was the chart locker, wide narrow drawers in which hundreds of charts could be stored flat and dry. From the navigator's pull-out seat, George could communicate through the open companionway with the helmsman in a conversational tone.

The fog had thinned only moderately, and as we headed out the starboard channel we hunted for telltale buoys that would confirm our position safe in navigable water—first on radar, then by eyesight. The mate would call out a description of the buoy we needed—red "nun," black or green "can," red or green bell-buoy—to the midships lookout, who relayed it to

---

* VHF is used for "line of sight" communications up to about 20 miles; SSB is for much longer range communications using the ionosphere for bouncing radio waves over the horizon, often more than 1000 miles. [Captain George Moffett's note]

Dean way out on the bow. Dean, tall and tan and bearded, blond hair braided down his back to his waist, leaned into the wind like an Indian scout and never failed to spot a marker first. He was a fitting figurehead, somehow, orange and blue-flowerd aloha shirt billowing in the wind made by our engine, hair streaming out behind, one hand raised to his brow to screen out the overcast glare.

Soon the museum dock was out of sight behind us, and we had left the channel island and its two lighthouses on our port quarter. Fog surrounded us, clearing every few minutes to reveal a docked container ship, a building, a chunk of green rugged shoreline, framing it for just an instant, then closing around it again. All about us was sound—other ships, bells, the clatter of heavy machinery on shore, automobile engines, voices, even squawking gulls. It was eerie, not the way I had envisioned the start of our passage at all. I had imagined a brisk tack in a freshening wind chilled by the Labrador Current. The air was heavy and wet, the wind was all wrong, and we had to rely on engine power instead of sails.

But we were all glad to be going, excited to be heading offshore.

Departing Halifax, N.S.
(Author's photo)

Dave took the wheel and George called out the course from the navigation station at the foot of the companionway. We ran at over six knots with a fair current to the harbor mouth, past The Sisters, the treacherous rocks guarding the western channel. Then we rounded Mars Rock and, in a few hours, Pennant Point, which indeed dangles like a pennant off the southern tip of the fat promontory of Greater Halifax. The current turned foul enough to knock a knot off our speed for the next six hours.

A cold lunch of sandwiches and fruit was late because we were all occupied with running out of the harbor, a dozen miles or so, and none of the crew seemed to notice. B-watch took over at one o'clock, and I clambered out onto the bowsprit to take the pulpit lookout. As we neared the open sea, the air had turned chiller, damper, and I had already changed into jeans and my fisherman's sweater. The rolling motion of the bow made me cautious as I made my way across the footropes, but in a few seconds I was aboard the pulpit and relaxing with the motion.

From my log:

> *For a good long time today, at various intervals, I rode the "widowmaker," as the bow lookout responsible to keep track of traffic and hazards and spot buoys coming out of harbor. At first you hold on tightly with both hands, then you get used to the regular motion and no longer need your hands. The sensation, as you lean forward and balance your weight against the rail at your stomach, is one of flying over the water.*
>
> *Free flight.*
>
> *You are way out ahead of everyone. They are lost somewhere behind you —out of sight, out of earshot, out of mind [this is an illusion, of course: the minute your eyes spot the ghost of a shape, you instinctively sing out to the midships lookout and your arm automatically swings up like a railroad semaphore to point out the object]. If you lean forward, you can't even see your feet. You can pretend there is nothing holding you down, you are weightless and airborne. Absolutely airborne.*
>
> *It is always colder on the bow, with no deck structures, no sails, no thick masts to block the wind. Coldest on the bowsprit, where the lookout rides totally exposed to wind and spray.*
>
> *Your stomach thrills the way it does on a carnival ride. It is just plain fun.*
>
> *The bow wave makes music against the hull, sliding off in a lulling whoosh.*

Once out of congested water, porpoises crossed our bows again and again—a favorable portent. Off to port, George spotted a pod of whales, too far away for ready identification. Probably humpbacks, though, as they were common in these waters at this season.

Captain George had a mariner's eye, that keenness of vision that is part natural gift, part practice, and part knowing what to look for. The kind of vision that is sharpened by other senses: listening into the fog for the clang of a bell buoy or the beat of an engine, feeling the motion of current and sea under you. Joshua Slocum, who sailed the world round as master of square-riggers such as *Northern Light*—whose mainmast was so tall, the story goes, that as she passed under Brooklyn Bridge a workman leaning down from his scaffold painted her masthead—once claimed that by looking at the color of the water, listening to the wind chafe through the rigging, and feeling the swell under his keel he could tell within a few miles his whereabouts on any ocean in the world. That kind of vision.

Captain George Moffett was trim and tanned, a handsome man who might be twenty-five or forty, with a thick shock of sandy hair. He moved on deck with an easy step, a practice of balance. He looked athletic in a casual sort of way—someone who wouldn't make a fuss about working out but who might murder you at tennis or racquetball without breaking a good sweat.

He spoke with a New Englander's accent, though he came from, of all places, the suburbs of Chicago. He lived in England for eight years and spoke German for two years while living in Bonn—long enough to lose any trace of the Midwest from his voice.

His grandfather, naval aviation pioneer Admiral William A. Moffett, had once been Commandant of the Great Lakes Naval Training Center on Lake Michigan, near the Wisconsin border. One of George's earliest sailing adventures, in fact, occurred on the lake while he was still a boy. George's father was delivering a new sloop from Winnetka up to the base at Great Lakes. The owner was aboard. George crewed. A line squall bore down on them from the west, across the shore. His father, a second generation Annapolis man, managed to douse all sails before the squall hit, but the little centerboard sloop was capsized anyway by the sheer force of the wind. Father and son spent three hours in the cold water clinging to the turtled hull before the Coast Guard rescued them.

George did not affect the salty costume of the Sunday sailor. Mostly he wore khaki trousers, topsiders, and flannel or chamois shirts. His sailing hat, acquired in Newport, Rhode Island, was a light canvas panama with a floppy brim. He attached it to a shirt button with a length of cord.

He rarely raised his voice, even on the raw edge of fogbound hours without good sleep. He commanded quietly, through suggestion and example, and trusted his crew. He handled the kids with a kind of paternal good nature. There was something of a born teacher about him, the urge not just to do a thing well but, once he saw you were interested, to teach you how to do it well, too. Not long ago he had been the headmaster of an English school, with recreation time spent cruising the English coast and the Channel, then venturing as far afield as the Mediterranean, the Red Sea, and East Africa. He was easy to like, and he exuded the strong sense that he had it all under control—the course, the ship, the crew.

The wind continued to blow in our faces, and there was no prospect of raising sail until the wind backed, that is, shifted counterclockwise, enough that we could make a rhumbline down the coast of Nova Scotia close-hauled. "We could tack back and forth under sail," George explained, spreading out his chart on the cockpit sole, "but it would add over a hundred miles to our trip." Twelve or more hours of sailing, in other words, depending on the number of tacks we'd have to make. He opened up the matter for discussion —he believed in the crew taking part in important navigation decisions, under his guidance—and we all agreed it made sense to continue under power until we could enjoy some real sailing in a good steady wind.

27

So we got used to the throb of the engine, the constant noise and vibration below decks.

Actually, owing to the particular design and installation of *Brilliant*'s 97-horsepower G.M.C. diesel and its engine room, noise and discomfort belowdecks were minimal. The midships head door, for one thing, doubled as the main saloon forward door, and could be closed and latched, confining the characteristic diesel roar to the forward sections—galley, captain's cabin, and fo'c'sle.

But more important was the ingenious plan of the engine room itself. Mr. Barnum had balked at the notion of locating the engine aft, under the cockpit—a location that had seemed logical to plenty of naval architects ever since the dawn of so-called "auxiliary sailing yachts" because of the proximity to the propeller. An engine located thus required a shorter shaft, could be serviced from the cockpit lazarettes (storage compartments), and could be segregated from sleeping quarters.

In his own thorough and unequivocal style, Barnum objected to placing the engine aft:

"As to layout," he wrote, "I have always felt most strongly on the subject of the usual plan of destroying that best of all storage places, the Lazarette, by installing therein an oily, smelly engine. Everything, in my opinion, is wrong with that idea. For the sake of a few square feet of space for the machine, you ruin pretty nearly all the cubic space in that area, either by cutting it up or by leaving it open with the engine compartment."

Brilliant's cast bronze floors in way of the fuel tank-engine bed assembly. (Rosenfeld Collection, Mystic Seaport Museum.)

His main objections, however, were even more practical than aesthetic:

"It is not the right place for that weight. If the engine is off center, you do not get the best foundation. The shape of the space makes working around the engine difficult, even when you are generous in the amount of space appropriated."

In addition, he pointed out, the worst of the vibration and noise would be that much closer to the helmsman, and fireproofing an engine in that close wooden compartment would be difficult.

"I would rather go without an engine altogether," he wrote, "than have one which could in any way destroy the sweetness of the air in any other part of the boat, or leak oil into the bilges."

His answer was to install the engine amidships, directly over the keel for stability, in a spacious compartment whose sides and ceiling were lined with heavy sheet aluminum. Remarkably, the original gasoline engine bed and fuel tank were cast *in one piece*, of half-inch-thick bronze, then tested with gasoline under pressure for porosity. Two castings were done to get it right. Furthermore, the floors under the bronze tank were also cast in bronze, for Barnum realized that wooden floor timbers under the engine would be impossible to inspect for wear and rot.

Brilliant's engine room was thus built as a self-contained, well-ventilated, well-lighted all-metal compartment, whose fuel, oil, and fumes could not contaminate any other part of the ship.

The original Kermath 4-cylinder gasoline engine was eventually replaced with a 6-cylinder 85-horsepower Gray marine gasoline engine, and that was lifted out in 1960 in favor of a G.M.C. diesel, deemed safer for nautical usage because diesel fumes are far less volatile than gasoline fumes. The new engine was mounted on the old foundation, allowing 130 gallons of diesel fuel to be stored in the under-engine bronze tank, affording *Brilliant* a considerable cruising range under power at a top speed of 7½ knots. *Brilliant* is now on her second diesel.

Late in the afternoon, some eighteen miles southeast of Lunenburg, Nova Scotia, the captain shut down the engine momentarily to adjust the propeller shaft sleeve. I was in the middle of my first trick at the helm. Suddenly the water next to the cockpit boiled and there he was—angular dorsal fin cutting the water in classic *Jaws* fashion. Shark. He stood by, slithery and menacing and in no apparent hurry, and the crew leaned over the bulwarks for a better look. He looked like a great white and, gauging his length alongside the cockpit, about ten feet long. He swam along with us as, without power, we slowly lost way. The repair done, we resumed power speed, and he kept with us only a few minutes before disappearing into the deep.

From my personal log, 2045 hours:

> Just came off watch a few minutes ago and oh, what a day! For almost the whole day we motored hard for Cape Sable, to get around Nova Scotia, which sticks out into the North Atlantic like a big down-turned thumb, and onto a sailing tack that takes us toward Nantucket. So we made a motor passage through fog and raw weather in big ground swells with the wind square on the nose and building. The crew are mostly subdued—waiting for better weather, and for a sailing wind. Especially Mike, who seems to have a touch of mal de mer *and keeps to his bunk off-watch. Not so Michelle, who came on board toting a copy of Conrad's* Heart of Darkness—*ambitious summer reading for her senior English class. I don't think she has managed to do much reading, but she has been a bright and cheerful presence, always the first volunteer for prep and cleanup duties in the galley.*
>
> At about 1730 George decided the wind was backing enough to motor sail, which we did for awhile, until the wind gave way to us and the engine, at long last, was shut down. And with it went, at long last also, the slight nausea that seems to be caused by the combination of long slow rollers hitting bow-on and the constant engine-throb.
>
> The jackstaff with its Stars & Stripes is unshipped—otherwise it will interfere with the overhang of the long main boom.
>
> Two sailors haul on the main halyard, leading it onto the mast-mounted winch for increased purchase, one pair of hands grinding the winch while the other pair tails the halyard and makes it off on the belaying pin at the foot of the mast with a fast half-hitch. After sail is raised, three other sailors sheet in the mains'l—one tailing, a second overhauling the sheet between boom and mastblock (never between block and winch), and a third standing by with winch handle ready to grind in the last few difficult feet.
>
> Watching the sails go up, from aft forward, is indeed a sight. The first time you see that enormous mains'l slide up the pole is a little breathtaking. It seems so big, rising off the deck like a great white wall, almost a thousand square feet of snow-white Dacron, winching into a flat curve against the dirty sky.

At the helm you can feel the ship heel over and the deep keel bite, tracking true. Each sail—fores'l, lapper jib, fisherman stays'l—adds steadiness to the helm, and the digital speedo creeps up from 5.3 knots under power alone to 7.5 knots.

After the engine is shut down, we maintain our speed with slight variation.

Like all true sailboats, Brilliant *is built not to power but to sail. She is at her best under sail, holding much better to the helm, and, cocked over 15 degrees or so, rolls less in the ocean swell.*

Doug, the mate, gave us a lesson in sail handling today. When you step aboard a schooner, her two masts and bowsprit and all that rigging at first seem like a complex tangle. You despair of ever being able to master all those lines and winches. But you go at it one sail at a time, aft to forward, for balance, and a certain intricate order reveals itself. Not simplicity by any stretch, not in the conventional sense, but the net result is a kind of elegant balance between hull and sails, wind and water.

The schooner rose to prominence in the first place for two reasons: speed on the wind, and simplicity of rig. If that sounds a bit hard to believe in a time when the aluminum-masted sloop has come to dominate our thinking about speedy, simple sailboats, the problem is one of perspective. As in most matters historical, to understand the "why" of it you cannot merely look backward in time; you have to look backward beyond the phenomenon, and then look forward from there.

Remember that the forerunner of the schooner was the square-rigger, in particular what we would now call a brig. The brig, formerly a pure square-rigger of two masts, foremast and main, developed by the nineteenth century into what is called a *hermaphrodite brig*—that is, the mainmast was rigged fore-and-aft.

A square-rigged sail limits a vessel's ability to sail on the wind, that is, with the wind coming from forward of the beam. A true square-rigged ship sails best with the wind pushing from behind it—that is, running or reaching —and therefore is best adapted to sail *with* the steady trade winds.

By contrast, a modern production sloop, which can pinch to within better than 45 degrees of the wind, is propelled by lift as the wind passes across the two sides of the bowed sail, the same as an airplane wing. The lift is translated into forward motion by the lateral resistance of the keel. It can sail anywhere, or almost anywhere, never mind wind direction.

This is, of course, a simplification, as Captain George explains: "The square-rigger also used its square sails for 'lift' when close-reaching with yards fully braced. The square sails then acted as airfoils, as with fore-and-aft sails, but not as efficiently."

And square-riggers need yards, lifts, braces, stays, and masts stout enough to carry it all—in short, a complicated and heavy rig requiring a large crew. On the old square-riggers, the sails were set from the yards by the crew high above the deck, a dangerous and labor-intensive business—especially so before the advent of the modern geared winch and steam-powered windlass.

Until the 1850s, many American schooners carried one or more square sails to complement their principal fore-and-aft sails. The pure form of the

33

schooner rig carried no awkward yards and was capable of having all working lower sails set from on deck, with relatively few hands required aloft to set tops'ls and stays'l. The rig could be adapted to hull size. In the second half of the nineteenth century the increasingly large hulls sprouted more masts. From three-masters grew four-, five-, six-, and even one seven-master, the latter being six times the length and 150 times the tonnage of *Brilliant*, though she operated with a crew of only eighteen.

Europe had its own schooner tradition. The schooner as a yacht became a standard after the schooner yacht *America* crossed the Atlantic to best the Royal Yacht Squadron in 1851. While the ketch or yawl had begun to supersede the schooner as an ocean-racing rig by the time *Brilliant* was built, she has continued to uphold her heritage.

Brilliant's sails are Dacron, weighing less than the original Egyptian cotton sails and but a fraction of wet cotton; still, setting the main requires at least three hands. Imagine the weight of a wet *cotton* mains'l if the foremast were eliminated and the area of the fores'l were added to the main (making a sloop) —it would be unmanageable without a large crew, the very thing the schooner was designed to eliminate.

So the schooner developed as a handy working boat, carrying cargo, notably fish, lumber, and coal. A fast coasting vessel whose windward ability made it equally maneuverable in the tradewinds, the variables, and the local breezes of harbors, bays, and lakes. And even a large overbuilt schooner, unlike a square-rigger of the same tonnage, could be handled safely and efficiently by a relatively small crew.

When the schooner found her way to the fishing industry, she also became a racing boat, probably the same way the skipjack and the sailing canoe did—by the necessity of beating the competition to market.

Back to the log:

The bowsprit is a bobbing needle against the horizon. The sails hold their shapes like glazed ceramic wedges as evening settles over the water. A hole in the fog has cleared around us, allowing, for the time being, a visibility of two miles or more. The sky is dirty with weather in all directions but north. But we are heading 260 degrees—west by south—toward Brazil Rock. Fast.

4

★ ★ ★

Brazil Rock to Cape Sable

Midnight in the open sea. It was time for the mate's watch to go on deck, so said Dean with a gentle nudge to my shoulder. I had napped for only an hour or so, still too fascinated by the novelty of sailing blue water to leave the deck for very long. At sea, with the settee often occupied, the chart table in continuous use, and the sea-berths on the high or weather side made precarious and uncomfortable by the constant heel of the boat, we shared "hot-bunks." The watch coming off duty simply hopped into the most convenient comfortable bunks—often still warm from the previous occupants.

I opened my eyes and peeled off the blankets. Down below my midships berth it was quiet. The captain talked in low tones with the helmsman, correcting the course by a Loran fix from time to time. His face and hands caught the rosy glow of the nightlamp over the chart table. At sea, we guarded our lights. Usually we moved about the cabin in the dark or with a flashlight so as not to ruin the navigator's night vision, or the night vision of any of the crew on watch. Once a bright light has been shined into the eyes, it takes precious minutes to recover night vision.

The radar screen glowed green, and amber digits showed on the Loran. I hopped down onto the settee and then to the cabin sole, used the head, and dressed. It was already cool, air temperature hovering around 65 degrees. But the clinging mist and the 10-knot wind made it positively cold. I pulled on wool socks over cotton socks, and over my skivvies thick sweatpants and jeans, and sweater. Then I stepped into my seaboots and yellow storm pants, zipped up my sou'wester, and put on my wool fisherman's cap.

In the near dark, the others were dressing. As soon as I had wriggled into my safety harness, I climbed up the companionway and stretched my legs on deck. Clint had the helm. He was, for once, without his customary pipe—his own choice, since smoking was allowed on deck but not below.

Mike appeared on deck right behind me and took the first half-hour trick at the wheel, and we began our rotation. Custom and the kind regard of your shipmates dictate that you come on watch promptly and, if possible, a few minutes early. Nothing can excite resentment quite so quickly on shipboard as failing to relieve the watch on time—those extra minutes always seem the longest, especially at night, in the cold, in a mist so thick it drenched us like rain.

"Watch" is an accurate word for deck duty, for each of us was always watching something. The mate navigated and made frequent sorties on deck, watching the weather, what he could see of it, and checking the trim of the sails by flashlight. (Doug wore glasses, a double liability in the fog: he had to continually wipe the mist off the lenses in order to see clearly.)

The rest of us took half-hour turns at each of four stations: the lookout went to the bow (with the choice of riding the pulpit or hunkering on solid deck behind the scant windbreak of the bulwarks) and watched the seas ahead for hazards, traffic, whatever was out there; the radarman stood over the navigator's shoulder and kept an eye on the radar screen, periodically adjusting the range and "sea-clutter" for an accurate scan of what lay in the ocean around us, including weather systems; the signalman stood by (or rather sat over) the foghorn button, located on the back of the cockpit well just beneath the lazarette cover, and watched the fast hand of a watch, every sixty seconds sounding a blast that would wake the holy dead, or at least anybody trying to sleep in the fo'c'sle; and the helmsman, of course, watched the glowing binnacle to keep the ship on her right course—for the time being, 245 degrees, or nearly west southwest.

From my log:

> The wind is steady from the south but dropping. The fog is thicker than ever, so dense that the forward running lights hardly seem to glow, so dense that from the cockpit the bow lookout is often invisible, only fifty feet away.
>
> By the time I come aft to relieve Liesel at the horn, Clint is serving up hot coffee. We wrap our hands around the steaming mugs gratefully. He is off watch, and so this is beyond the call of duty. Clint's coffee, strong and piping hot, pumps up our flagging morale, clears the sand out of our eyes so we become as alert as we need to be during this tricky leg of the passage.
>
> Liesel goes below to stand by radar, Mike makes his way forward to drink his coffee at the bow, and Dean slides in behind the wheel. It is always the freshest hand who takes the wheel—the one who has warm fingers.
>
> The captain has not turned in, mainly because we will soon pass Brazil Rock, which sticks up way offshore and is invisible, except for the radar buoy. He confers with Doug at the navigation station, and we sail on, feeling the heavy motion of the ship in the diminishing wind.

It was Brazil Rock which had provided some excitement on *Brilliant*'s Marblehead to Halifax race only the week before. In a dense fog, George was navigating to pass very close to the Brazil Rock radar buoy and, by confirming the buoy, make a precise Loran check, when all of a sudden there it was, dead ahead and closing fast. A quick maneuver to starboard was necessary to pass on the safe side of the buoy.

The culprit turned out to be the radar unit, or rather how that unit was mounted on the mainmast. Apparently, for reasons unknown, the radar had been knocked out of true and was now reporting a 10-degree error to starboard. That is, anything 10 degrees to port was actually dead ahead. Remedying the problem would entail a prolonged adventure aloft for one of the crew while George read the screen against an absolutely known landmark—impossible to do while we were at sea.

Once we knew to make the correction, using the radar was fairly easy.

We plough ahead through zero visibility for four hours. No stars can be seen overhead. The water is audible chafing along our waterline, but all we can see of it is a head of white foam directly in our wake, lit by the white stern running light. We are getting used to the chafe of the hull through the water, of the wind through the rigging. When the sound of things alters, even slightly, conversation stops automatically and we listen hard, staring into the fog in the direction of the change, as if that will focus our ears.

Like as not when that happens, Doug will pop out of the companionway, flashlight in his fist, to inspect the sail trim and speculate about the weather. He'll lean there in the cockpit for a few minutes, in an old hard-used yellow reefer and navy watchcap, just making sure everything's all right.

My foul weather gear is drenched, but underneath it I am warm and dry and tired. I should have slept more in the early evening. We are a subdued lot, talking by fits and starts in the cockpit, joshing about sea monsters and uncharted rock islands out there in the fog.

Well before his watch is to begin, Clint comes on deck. Clint, who never seems to sleep and spends much of his time perched on the ladder of the midships scuttle, elbows draped over the step, pipe in mouth. Visible from the chest up, a head and shoulders figure looking absolutely content. Clint has extraordinary sea-legs; he moves about the ship rarely holding on, as the rest of us do reflexively on such a severe heel. He is not showing off, or making a point, unless it is to himself. He just seems to be one of those rare creatures of unnatural balance.

As for myself, I am already sore and bruised in odd places—on the elbows, knees, hips, the fronts of my thighs—from stumbling into the hard edge of the main saloon table, being jostled onto bunk boards, barking shins against the companionway ladder, tripping over deck gear in the dark. As time goes on, I move in and on the terrain of the ship more confidently, feeling her motion as naturally as my own heartbeat.

Even George and Doug have admitted to new bruises the first night at sea after a long shore leave.

In the cockpit, Clint and Doug are talking about container ships. "I read somewhere," claims Doug, "that this one container ship lost twenty containers off her deck in a storm. Twenty. Just bobbing around, waiting to stove somebody."

"They probably sank," says Clint, and I'm relieved. "Then again, maybe not. If they were sealed right . . ." He fusses with his pipe.

"Corvettes. Cars. That's what was in them. One Corvette to a box."

"Imagine running down one of those on a night like this. Wouldn't even show up on radar."

"No, I guess it wouldn't. Would look just like wavetops." On the radar screen, most of the "sea-clutter" is breaking wave tops. If a blip appears and then disappears at random, you can tell it is nothing solid, nothing to worry your pretty hull.

"You'd see it," I say. "The blip wouldn't go away."

"Oh," says Doug in his best downeaster voice, "they'd be half-submerged, I guess. Might not see 'em 'tall."

This goes on and on. The best thing about the night watch is the voices, the easy talk against the rush of water. This, I imagine, is what I came for. The weather is indeed foul, and we are all tired and edgy in the fog, but the talk is always good. The voices carry the authority of reassurance, the insistent reminder that we are all in this together, the safety of human company.

On board, at night, it was always the talk. We are most of us brought up not to speak unless we have something to say. Our heroes of screen and literature are taciturn and monosyllabic, men of few words, who speak only to get something said. Tight-lipped Yankees, whose conversation is only functional, a means to an end.

But the talk on board during those long night watches (for no night watch is ever short) was an older kind of talk: talk for the pure sound of it. For the murmur of voices introduced into the sea and wind and sky a human element—the way that a human figure, a posing tourist say, can lend a comforting perspective to a snapshot of the Grand Canyon, without diminishing its grandeur even a mite. Rather, the little human reminds us of outrageous scale, acts as a foil to the giant.

With the puny human as a yardstick, we can finally imagine grandeur that, otherwise, simply boggles our imagination.

Our soft voices filled the nighttime. Voices. We talked just to hear ourselves talk, never mind what was said. What was said was generally so unremarkable that, to repeat it precisely, I'd have to reinvent it—jokes about Newfies (Newfoundlanders), memories of other boats, other passages, off-hand comments about the weather, the sails, the fog, the breeze.

Should we crank in the main just a tad, or leave it be?

I was aboard a schooner once that was rammed during a race, Clint says, her cabinhouse stove in by a splintering bowsprit.

There's a front moving in, just look at the radar.

Will we see the sun tomorrow? Sure, maybe. Or maybe not.

Repetition, desultory and mundane snatches of conversation, connected only by the tone—muted, amiable, intimate. Miles offshore, safe in a net of voices. Campfire voices. Voices on a train long after midnight when all the other passengers, strangers, are nodding against their headrests. Voices of the grown-ups in the front seat of a car as they sound to one child in the backseat, still awake long after bedtime, who watches his parents' faces flicker in and out of shadow and the brief illumination of oncoming headlights.

The kind of murmuring, pointless voices that have got mankind through centuries of dark nights, and will always.

We talked whenever we felt like it. We listened. We made affirmative grunts and called softly each other's names when the time came to rotate to the next watch station: Liesel, Mike, Dean. It was all very primitive. It was all very civilized.

Back to the log:

Clint has had cornbread baking, and now shares it, still warm from the oven, around the cockpit. We eat and settle back to our watch.

It is a little daunting to know we are miles beyond any landed horizon, even if we could see to the horizon. And we are heading still farther. Once we round the tip of Nova Scotia, we will strike out directly across the Gulf of Maine and be well over a hundred miles from shore. This is new. This is just the ship now out of any context but the one she knows best, blue water.

I recall our safety drill, the man-overboard scenario, at night, in fog. I check and double check my safety harness, which I wear (we all wear) even in the cockpit, in case we were to get pooped by a following sea—unlikely, but so are all hazards, until they happen.

The captain (I think) is catching some sleep. We are sailing blind, have been for hours. But we have a good radar—our "star chart." We scan up and down the range and watch the blips of wave tops come and go. Six range settings are available: for ½, 1, 2, 4, 8, and 12 miles in a compass around our ship. The scope is calibrated in four concentric rings, so that, for instance, at range 12 miles the distance between rings is 3 miles; at a range of 1 mile the distance between rings is ¼ mile, and so on.

The screen is spattered with green blips. When the spattering is too dense, we adjust the sea-clutter knob and filter out the mask of wave tops. Now we can spot hard blips, fishing boats and ships, passing us miles away. We track them across our scope. The navigator, at intervals, notes their position and progress out loud to the helmsman, who in turn alerts the lookout.

And we have our Loran, with its radio-beamed frequencies unscrambled by compact, solid-state electronics into numbers which, applied to the chart, indicate just where we are on this blank and foggy ocean. It even reads us the course we are making and, once the navigator has programmed in our next destination point, it displays the most favorable course to follow.

We have the radiotelephones with which to call any other vessel, the Coast Guard, or any shore station in range.

But, in some important way, all this twentieth-century gadgetry is beside the point. Because what we really have is a good boat under us, and what we really have is Captain George's seamanship. That is what we rely on. We rely on his experience at sea delivering a trawler from England to Djibouti, East Africa, and exploring the French and English coasts for six years in his 1927 ketch, and cruising these northeastern shores for many seasons—testing and building on his knowledge of the intricacies of piloting, navigation, and boat-handling. Practical knowledge, of the head and the hands.

In that sense we are no different from any sailing ship that ever ventured out of harbor. We are many hands and strong backs and eyes to watch, but the miracle of the voyage is that behind all the complex electronics, all the tangle of lines and sheets and rigging, is a governing intelligence. A single mind keeps us sailing. The good judgment of the captain keeps a 42-ton wooden ship on a true course, sails drawing to maximum advantage, all the machines and people on board cooperating to produce a single, efficient line of distance made good across the chart.

Clint said it: the wind comes from somewhere, you work the sails, and the boat goes somewhere. Simple. But it is a mind that harnesses all the independent efforts, the force expended in many divergent directions, into one direction: forward.

Sometime during the waning hour of watch we leave Brazil Rock and its aberrant danger eleven miles west by north. Shortly thereafter we retire. I am so done in that, after I shed my storm gear, I scramble into my bunk fully clothed, and sleep deeply and without dreaming.

As I dropped off I heard the foghorn and, in between, voices. Michelle at the wheel laughing quietly at some remark. Dave's deep, steady voice. George, apparently rested, asking the helmsman to come up three degrees. "Steady," he said, "All right. That's a good course. Just hold her there awhile."

5

★ ★ ★

Cape Sable
Across the Gulf of Maine

Fog. The prevailing south southwest wind in these parts blew warm air over the cold Labrador Current as it carried us south, and the inevitable result was fog. At 0800 the mate's watch came on deck and I took the wheel. Sometime during the night we had passed off Cape Sable, the jutting tip of Nova Scotia, and we were making a generally westerly course now, correcting by south or north to maintain our route. We were crossing the vast Gulf of Maine, open water. We sounded the foghorn as we neared the fishing banks or spotted another vessel on radar, saving the old horn compressor motor from complete exhaustion.

On deck, nothing had changed except that the fog was now translucent, backlighted by a sun we could not see. Though we all said the fog could not possibly last much longer, visibility would never be much better than zero for the next twenty-four hours. We had no way of knowing now that the fog stretched all the way down the coast to Mystic.

From my log:

"I don't believe this," Doug says over and over of the fog. We have been at sea now for a day and a night, and all of us are tired. Doug doesn't look rested, but he goes about his duties as usual—moving between the deck and the navigation station, checking sail trim, watching the weather, such as it is, sniffing for wind.

"I don't sleep well with the engine off," he confesses. "I keep waiting for something to crash through the hull." He laughs when he talks about it. He tossed and turned with his eyes wide open most of the night, he admits. His concern is not exactly a rational one, yet it is not entirely irrational, either. The American merchant marine, for instance, discontinued the practice of housing crews in the fo'c'sle earlier this century because so many men were dying in collisions. Sleeping aboard a ship underway in dense fog is chancier than snoozing in your bed at the Holiday Inn.

In your bunk, you can hear the water rushing by only a few inches from your head. Between you and it are only teak planks, fitted there half a century ago. You hear odd bumping noises under the hull as Brilliant surfs down a wave or jumps a cross sea.

You hear occasional commotion on deck even through the thick overhead. Footsteps in a hurry. A suddenly loud voice calling down the companionway. Someone getting up and, half asleep, stumbling forward in the dark to find the head. The rattle of pans from the galley.

And Doug is, by nature, a worrier. That, I suppose, is part of what makes him so valuable to this ship: he does not assume all is well. He checks. He makes sure. Is that sheet chafing? Are the bilges dry? How does the fores'l set? What's the wind doing? Anything on radar at four miles? At twelve? Then after he has made sure once and for all, he double-checks. He wants no surprises. He is fond of what NASA likes to call "redundant systems" —backups for backups.

A sailing ship is a dynamic floating system contrived of a thousand details: this one has, for instance, a foremast (rising 65 feet above the water), a mainmast (80 feet), two booms, and a bowsprit from which to fly sails; halyards for jib, forestays'l, and mains'l, as well as throat and peak halyards for fores'l and fisherman stays'l, or seven halyards altogether; two running backstays; sheets, outhauls, and downhauls for every sail, as well as a Cunningham for the main; seventeen winches with detachable handles (easily lost overboard) to manage this assortment of lines; a double windlass forward to handle two anchor chains at once; the engine and all its accessories; batteries, gauges, and a bank of electronic gadgets. Any item of gear might fail at any time; the consequences might be trivial, or they might be disastrous.

Mate Doug Butler keeps an eye on the rigging. (Author's photo)

Three men have commanded *Brilliant* during her thirty-five years at Mystic Seaport. They are: Captain Adrian Lane (right), 1953–61; Captain Francis Bowker (left), 1962–83; and Captain George Moffett, 1984–. (Photo by Claire White-Peterson)

And perhaps most important and unpredictable is the human factor—a crew of varied experience brought together as a team only by the patience and skill of the captain and mate.

A good part of Doug's job is teaching.

This crew is different from the ones Brilliant *is used to. Ordinarily, from June to September she sails with all-teenage crews as part of the Mystic Seaport Sail Education Program, courses in seamanship and sail-handling. This she has done for thirty-five years under three different skippers: Captain Adrian Lane (1953–1961), Captain Francis E. "Biff" Bowker (1962–1983), and since 1984 Captain George Moffett, who served as mate for a time under Bowker.*

More than five thousand teenagers over the years have gone for a cruise on the Brilliant. *In fact, among our crew, Liesel will remain in Mystic after this passage to serve as a youth counselor aboard the* Joseph Conrad, *headquarters for the program. For the past four or five years, the first and last cruises in* Brilliant's *annual season of 20-odd cruises have been for all-adult crews.*

Our crew, then, is a hybrid. At first, the kids were disappointed to see so many adults on board. Upon joining the ship at Halifax, Michelle said, in her characteristic straightforward fashion, "This is it? No more kids? How are we going to have any fun?"

Now it turns out to be a pretty good mix. We adults provide a certain steadiness, and the kids keep us from taking ourselves too seriously. When we are all on watch together we don't think of them as "kids"—we trust them to handle their jobs. And they do, eagerly, and without complaint.

We sail on through fog and calm seas, having lost all track of time. If a Viking longboat were to rear its dragon-headed prow on our beam, we would not find it remarkable. The Norsemen believed that those fearsome figureheads would help them find their way in a strange sea; we have radar, our dragon's eyes.

The watch drags on, and the temperature has slid down into the fifties. A head cold has sabotaged my equilibrium, and my ears are rushing with sound. The effect is to make me very drowsy and to make being belowdecks unpleasant.

At last it was one o'clock. As was customary, the new watch ate first, before relieving us. We went below, shed our storm pants and jackets, and hung them to dry either in the starboard locker at the foot of the companion-way or else on the dogging screws of the ports. Then we sat down for a lunch of cold cuts and chicken soup before hitting the sack.

As always, I had a healthy appetite. I ate heartily at every opportunity, grabbed every cup of coffee, apple, and chocolate that was passed my way, and still I lost seven pounds—more than a pound a day.

The new watch cleared the table and scrubbed the dishes—the idea, a very sensible one, being that the watch coming off should be exempt from any chore more arduous than climbing into a bunk.

A teenage crewmember
at the wheel, 1985.
(Photo by Pam Lott)

For the first time in my life, because of the head cold for which I had no pharmaceutical remedy and because I knew it would knock me right out, I took a seasickness pill. Unlike Doug, I slept well and deeply, to awake rested and clear-headed six hours later, be the first one dressed for deck watch, and relieve Michelle at the helm a few minutes early.

A-watch went below, and for a precious few minutes I had the deck to myself. Installed comfortably behind the wheel, legs braced on either side of the steering shaft, I held her easily at 258 degrees, west by south, never turning the wheel more than a spoke either way to keep the compass needle dead on. The fog had not thinned, but before me in the filtered twilight the whole deck was visible, bright at the edges. Here was this incredible power, all the physics of a monstrously tall rig coordinated to take the force of the Atlantic wind and harness it to work a 42-ton hull forward exactly where we wanted it to go, and I could control it all with one light hand on the wheel.

Like the helmsmen on the old square-riggers, who looked not ahead of them (their vision was blocked anyway by deck clutter and sails) but up and down, I kept my eye alternately on the compass and on the luff of the mains'l. The bowsprit stabbed into the fog ahead, and our white wake disappeared a few yards behind us. For now this was my ship, my passage. For the time it took the rest of my watch-mates to get dressed, it was my seamanship that mattered, my careful eye and hand that kept us on course, a glimpse into the wonderful and frightening responsibility of command at sea. A romantic illusion, to be sure, but there it was: for an extended moment, I sailed the ship alone through the fog. I might have been the only person left in the world.

It was a moment of the most magnificent loneliness you can imagine.

I had had that feeling only once before, years ago, on a highway that cut through the vast rangeland of West Texas. I had been driving all day, alone, my third day out of Delaware headed for Tucson, Arizona, and it dawned on me all at once that I hadn't seen another car for hours. Moreover, I could not for the life of me recall passing any stores, houses, barns, any of the evidence of people. I stopped the truck right there on the roadway. Why pull over? No one was coming in either direction for as far as the eye could see. I got out, stood on cramped and shaky legs, and listened.

No human sound reached me.

All I could hear was the fitful wind beating across the huge, open prairie —the most ancient sound in the world. It was the spookiest, most God-forgotten place I have ever been. For those minutes that I stood in the roadway, the sound of the prairie wind rushing in my ears, the landscape for a dozen miles around devoid of movement and barren of habitation, it was actually possible to believe that I was the last man on earth.

But at the wheel of *Brilliant*, however spooky the fog made everything seem, I could feel none of the panic I had felt that time in Texas, when I had hopped back in my old Datsun pickup and roared out of that place as fast as those little wheels could carry me. Instead I listened now to voices gathering in the companionway, kidding voices, voices full of comfort and good feeling, and greeted each by name as, one by one, they climbed on deck: Dean, Liesel, Mike, Doug.

They were all feeling better rested, tuned to the regular motion of the hull and the peculiar sensation of living in a house that was constantly tilted at a 15-degree angle.

By 10 P.M. (2200) the wind had risen to force 4, better than 11 knots, and light seas had replaced the calm. Our speed was up to nearly nine knots. We were fairly busting along in the fog and darkness, and had given up posting a bow lookout as an exercise in futility. Now we had a rest period in our cycle, and were doubly vigilant at the star chart.

Rested we were, but the relentless fog had Captain George and Doug on edge. Wind and seas continued to rise, but the wind was unable to blow away the fog. We had not seen a landmark in thirty-six hours. We had not sighted a star for two nights. We were sailing now on space-age instruments and old-fashioned instinct.

For me the fog, which had endured so long and now seemed more impenetrable than ever, lent a sense of other-worldliness to the passage. This was a kind of dream of sailing, with no external frame of reference. Oddly, though at times I felt fatigue swimming behind my eyes and the cold clammy breeze chilled me under all my layers of storm gear, I never worried much about the fog. I suppose that came of not having the responsibility of finding a safe route through it, and of trusting implicitly those who did.

Deck view looking forward, 1932. On the cabin top is a standard compass for taking bearings. The spinnaker pole is on deck, next to the sheet tackle for the staysail. (Rosenfeld Collection, Mystic Seaport Museum.)

6

★ ★ ★

91 mi. E of Cape Cod to Nantucket

At intervals throughout our second night at sea Captain George or Doug fired up the engine—not for speed, for we continued to charge along in force 4 and force 5 winds—but to recharge the batteries. Our constant use of radar, Loran, and the foghorn (which worked off a compressor) over such an extended period sapped the 32-volt system. Also, all wooden boats leak a little bit, and, *Brilliant* being no exception, on alternate watches we pumped out the bilge. Captain George wanted to have plenty of battery power for instrument piloting through Nantucket Sound.

Before the engine turned over, there sounded a five-second alarm bell, audible throughout the ship, followed by the shudder of all that horsepower cranking in its bronze bed.

On my rest cycle, just before midnight sent us off-watch, I went below with Captain George and stood by while he made an adjustment in the regulating apparatus of the charging mechanism to assure a more efficient charge from the engine. I was frankly amazed at his mechanical prowess— most of the sailors I know very nearly pride themselves on their ignorance of machines and engines, romantic to the point of foolishness about sail.

But Captain George, trained for two years at Annapolis as a naval engineer, seemed right at home in the engine room, as he had in the engine room of that oversized towboat at Halifax wharf. He had made his way between the two gargantuan Detroit diesels and asked pointed questions of the engineer: How could cooling be handled by such a small pump? Why were the engines mounted stern-to at such a radical ascending angle? How did the transmission box work?

In the din of his cabin, as he fooled with dials and knobs, Captain George explained the whole procedure. I watched and nodded, catching the gist but not the technical details, before going back on deck. In a few minutes we were snug in our bunks, listening to the engine sounds muffled by the bulkheads, feeling the low vibration in the planks at our elbows. Sometime soon after the engine shut down, its mechanical vibration replaced by the chafe of water against the hull—what nautical writers call the "chuckle" of the water—in my dreams, I felt it.

Doug slept better with the reassuring throb of the engine blocking out all other sea-sounds. Kept him, I guess, from imagining Krakens, Remora Monsters, whales, and uncharted rocks punching through the hull. I slept well either way.

In the night I felt us scrape bottom, felt our keel bump over something more solid than a wavetop, but could not be sure I wasn't only dreaming.

I don't know exactly what woke me. Perhaps it was the blast of the foghorn, which had been silent for so long, now coming at thirty-second intervals. Or the sound of anxious voices at the navigation station, followed by the thump of sea-boots pounding fast up the companionway. I slipped out of my bunk, the captain's bunk, in the stateroom. Doug was already up, alert and dressed. The captain stood by the radar and adjusted the sea-clutter. Clint was calling down from the cockpit: "Can't see him yet. Not yet."

On the radar scope was a large blip, just off the port bow, closing fast. Definitely a ship. We bore off, altering course to starboard—the standard maneuver dictated by the Rules of the Road in such a situation. The other vessel mimicked our maneuver, only seemed to alter course to port, and our relative headings remained the same. He was within a mile now, still closing.

We bore off again to starboard, and again the phantom vessel stayed with us. Captain George went halfway up the companionway to look out. Doug watched the radar. "There!" somebody shouted. "Two points off the port bow."

She passed within a hundred feet of us. A ketch under sail, a forty or fifty-footer. We were two vessels nearly a hundred miles off the nearest land, in two-foot seas and a freshening breeze and dense fog, and she had deliberately sailed within two boatlengths of us.

As she sailed by, two men in her cockpit waved.

"The other skipper was not sounding a horn, nor did he seem to be watching radar," Captain George recalled later. "We also tried three times to reach him on the radio. He seemed quite surprised to see and hear us."

The irony was immediately apparent: Had neither vessel been equipped with radar, we would have passed each other in the night and fog, safely oblivious with plenty of searoom between. On the other hand, it was our radar which had alerted us to the possible danger. Modern technology, so far as we were concerned, had in this instance canceled itself out.

I did not know it at the time, but later I learned that the *Stockholm* had rammed the *Andrea Doria* under just such circumstances. In thick fog off Nantucket, not far from where we encountered the ketch, each vessel was tracking the other on radar. Each deliberately changed from what would have been a safe course to avoid the other, with catastrophic results.

Now the scope was clear, I had a warm bunk to crawl back into, and A-watch had another two hours or so to mull over the identity of the other ship, the who and why and from where that could never be solved. Not in this fog.

From my personal log:

Four a.m. Zero visibility. Engine performs charging duties for an hour and a half. First the bell, then the thrum *of ignition and the steady vibration*

Brilliant's original gaff rig, 1932. (Rosenfeld Collection, Mystic Seaport Museum.)

along every plank in the ship. At my suggestion, Clint has added chocolate powder to the coffee. The result is an immediate hit: mocha-coffee, sweet and hot and satisfying.

The fog has lasted longer than any of us expected. It has strained our eyesight and our spirits, not to mention Captain George's nerves. Even he has never sailed this long a passage in continuous fog. The thing that went bump in the night was probably a whale, Dean tells me. We must have slid right over its back. The fog has all our imaginations working overtime, as we stare out into it and see only the weak white light of the stern lamp reflected back at us through millions of droplets of water. Air and water have become the same thing. While the engine is churning us through the nighttime fog, it is easy to imagine we are somehow on patrol, at risk, perhaps hunting submarines the way Brilliant *did for two years during World War II.*

Walter Barnum had kept *Brilliant* only seven years before he sold her, for personal reasons, to General Motors attorney Henry T. Bodman. Thus did *Brilliant* become, for three years or so before going off to the war, a Great Lakes cruiser out of Grosse Point, Michigan.

William W. Spivy's aunt, Emily Eaton, purchased *Brilliant* in Spivy's name in October 1942, with the express purpose of making her available to the Coast Guard for wartime service. Spivy himself served on *Brilliant* as Bosun's Mate 1st class until being detached in February of '44 to the Coast Guard Academy for officer's training. After receiving his commission, he was stationed first in Puerto Rico and later in the Pacific Theater on patrol boat duty, and never saw *Brilliant* again. When the Coast Guard returned *Brilliant* after the war, along with a sum of money to restore her to prewar condition, he authorized Sparkman & Stephens to find a buyer for her.

During the war, *Brilliant* operated from a base at the yacht club on St. Simon's Island, Georgia, as part of the Coast Guard Reserve's Coastal Picket Patrol. *Brilliant* and the fleet of power and sail craft pressed into service with her ("The Hooligan Navy"), many of them fine old yachts, were supposed to spot German submarines and function as a kind of early warning system against attack by sea.

Under the command of Captain Harry Peterson, and in company with the yacht *Evening Star* (now CGR 184), *Brilliant* made the passage from Detroit down to New York via Lake Erie and the Erie Barge Canal. At Buffalo, *Brilliant*'s topsides were repainted battleship gray and at the bows was stenciled her official designation as CGR 185. Her sticks were pulled and stored in cradles on deck, along with her booms, and some four weeks later she was rerigged at Far Rockaway, New York City.

A crew of six—including Peterson, Spivy, Motor Machinist's Mate William M. Lauhoff, Jr., a Bosun's Mate 2nd class, and two seamen—sailed *Brilliant* down the coast to Philadelphia, then south along the Inland Waterway to her station at St. Simon's Island. Two .30-caliber belt-fed machine guns were bolted to her teak decks, and Lauhoff remembers that a Thompson submachine gun and a rifle were also carried against the possibility of having to fight at close quarters, but were fired only in target practice.

"Our principal weapon was our radio, which worked beautifully," Spivy

opposite
Dropping the balloon staysail, ca. 1932. (Rosenfeld Collection, Mystic Seaport Museum.)

explained in an interview with George Moffett. "Our interest was not to *do* anything to a submarine, but to sight it and report it."

Lauhoff, now living in the Chicago area, agrees: "It was our job to spot, report the position, then get the hell out of there." He also remembers that there was little for a Machinist's Mate to do aboard *Brilliant* in those days besides routine maintenance—changing spark plugs and oil—for *Brilliant* patrolled under sail, using her engine only occasionally to make the twelve-mile channel into St. Simon's Yacht Club in an adverse wind. "The idea," Lauhoff explains, "was that the U-boats couldn't pick up any motor noise if we were under sail."

Like other picket craft, *Brilliant* patrolled a grid fifty miles square, ranging as far south as Savannah. Off Savannah, her lookouts sighted a sub and destroyers gave chase. Several more sightings were logged and reported between May 1942, when she went into action, and the end of the war.

According to Spivy, *Brilliant*'s usual routine was three days on patrol and three days off. Lauhoff recalls that on occasion the patrols lasted as long as a week. The original watch system, again according to Spivy, was four hours on, four hours off, with half the crew on watch at all times; before long, however, Captain Peterson realized how fatiguing that system was over a sustained period and modified it to a three watch system under which each crew member had four hours on and eight hours off—the off watch hours being a chance to catch up on both sleep and ship's maintenance.

Brilliant came through the war unscathed, though Lauhoff says he will never forget at least one harrowing experience aboard. Ironically, the incident occurred just as *Brilliant*, newly rerigged, was heading out of New York Bay. "There was supposed to be a pilot boat to guide us through the mines, since we had no charts." Repeated attempts to signal other craft were unsuccessful. "None of us on board could read semaphore—we had had no training, just volunteered because we were sailors. Finally a boat did come alongside, to tell us that now we were safely through the mines!"

Briggs Cunningham, the famous sailor whose name now denotes the grommet above the tack used to downhaul the mains'l and shape its luff for a better set (the "Cunningham"), bought *Brilliant* at auction after the war for $9,500 with an eye to racing her. He had her repainted to her original glossy white and rerigged, at a cost of about $75,000. To give her better speed in light airs, he had her masts made taller by nine feet to handle bigger sails.

But postwar technology and changes in measurement rules effectively closed out the era of the racing schooner, and after *Brilliant* finished at the back of the fleet in the 1946 Bermuda Race, she rarely left Long Island Sound until her subsequent donation by Cunningham to Mystic Seaport Museum, Inc.

So in the course of a colorful career, *Brilliant* has been bought four times and donated twice, finishing only a few miles up the coast from where she started fifty-five years ago, as one of only a handful of full-time sail-training vessels commissioned under the United States flag.

Briggs Cunningham, while extending her spars, had retained *Brilliant*'s double gaff rig (mains'l and fores'l). In 1958 the Seaport fitted her with a jib-headed main, for greater ease in handling with teenage crews: no more need

to raise a tops'l, a difficult and tricky drill. This advantage is offset, some maintain (including Captain Bowker), by an increased tenderness and the necessity of reefing the main in winds greater than force five. Bowker also says that the new rig slows her down when sailing wing-and-wing, that is, running before the wind with booms on opposite sides.

That four-to-eight watch was for me the longest of the passage, the last fog-bound watch, the culmination of forty-eight hours at sea. The logbook recorded the air temperature as 65–70 degrees, but by now I was wearing double socks under seaboots; undershorts, sweatpants, and jeans under storm lowers; t-shirt, thermal undershirt, sweater, and windbreaker under my reefer; wool fisherman's hat under a closely drawn hood; and wool Army surplus glove liners.

Clint served up more hot cornbread halfway through the watch and sat out on deck with us smoking when he had every right to be sound asleep and warm belowdecks.

Doug was on deck often, flashlighting the mains'l and wondering out loud how much longer it would be before we'd have to reef. Our heel had increased slightly, and all around us on the star chart were the massed blips of squalls. We went busting along in the center of a horseshoe of squalls, heading for the open side. We could see whitecaps on the weather beam. We watched lightning split the sky off to starboard, webbing the darkness even through the fog, then heard the report of thunder. We counted the seconds between flash and boom—ten seconds, one mile off for each seven. We kept counting, and they never got any closer.

On the radar scope, the squalls retreated north and east, slowly. We must be right on a major front, we figured. If that were true, we might get hit and hit hard before sunup. In any case, we were in for a change in the weather.

Doug brought a length of cord on deck and passed it among the watch. "Do you know how to tie a reef knot?" he asked each of us in turn—Liesel, me, and Mike. (He did not insult Dean by asking him, Dean being one of the Mystic Seaport shipyard's expert riggers who, among other special duties, has been called upon in the past to bend sail onto the yards of the whaleship *Charles W. Morgan*.)

I had tied reef knots before when shortening sail on my little cutter *Teddy Blue*, usually (but not always) at leisure and in daylight. Under Doug's direction, I practiced it again. It took me three tries to get it right. Some things are harder to do with an expert watching. I tied three more to make sure I could do it in the dark and quickly, should the occasion arise.

A reef knot, used to secure the lowered part of the mains'l to the boom and so leave less sail area exposed to the wind, ties the same as a square knot. In this case we learned to tie the reef knot with a slip, which means forming a bight with one of the ends before closing the knot. This loop projects out of the knot like half a shoelace knot; yank the loop, and the knot is untied. The reef knot has in common with most mariners' knots that it can be untied at least as easily as it can be tied, though this ease of undoing does not affect its holding ability. At sea, untying a knot quickly can be every bit as crucial as tying one quickly.

We all practiced till we had it right. It gave us something to do. Doug kept an eye on weather and sail trim, now and then wiping mist off his glasses. We would not reef, not yet.

The monotony of the fog was wearing us down. On the scope from time to time we spotted trawlers, all of them far away and bearing off. We yawned and told flat jokes and, joints stiff and eyelids heavy, kept the old ship jogging ahead on course.

Asleep in the starboard midships bunk, I was suddenly pitched against the leeboard and held there as the boat heeled hard onto the opposite tack. As soon as I could extricate myself, I climbed down and stuck my head out the companionway. The sun was shining in a cerulean sky, and a big wind was blowing. I would never call a sky that was merely blue "cerulean"; this sky was backlit into a uniform blue so thick and deep you could scoop it out and put it into a jar. The water reflected the sky.

In the time it took to slip on topsiders and sweater, I was on deck, for the first time since leaving Halifax harbor without foul weather gear.

Brilliant went spanking along through the blue water.

A teenage crewmember trims the jib, 1985. (Photo by Pam Lott)

From my log:

Everything has changed overnight. The fog has blown clean away, and the wind is piping up over 20 knots. I have been on deck for two hours, off-watch, feeling as rested and high-spirited as I ever have in my life.

Almost the whole crew is on deck by noon, and by the time I take the wheel the porpoises come back. One of them leaps so close across our bow that I wonder we did not hit him. They are all around us now, black and white arcs rising out of the blue water. Captain George attracts them by knuckling out signals on the hull. They swim over to investigate and cavort alongside for minutes at a time before suddenly heading off again, only to return in an endless playful cycle.

The weight of the fog has been lifted off us. My head cold is clearing. Doug's glasses are clear. The Canadian courtesy ensign is struck—we are in U.S. waters now.

I go forward to ride the bowsprit and keep a lookout, bobbing high and heeled over hard. We are still some thirty miles off Nantucket Sound when Captain George spots a pod of humpback whales way off to starboard. "You can see them by the misty puff when they blow," he says, pointing. And suddenly there they are, dozens of them, breaching and blowing all over the sea.

One of the whales breaches and sounds three times in succession, then pulls up close to the schooner and just lies there on the water, so that we get an astonishing sense of just how enormous is his (her?) black carcass. It is a stunning day.

All of us are laughing and hooting and crying out in sheer joy. This is our Nantucket sleighride, all right. The thrill of movement and release, sunshine over blue water, porpoises and whales on every point of the compass, the biggest wind we've had in days and holding.

Even George, an old hand in these waters, and Doug, who has crewed much larger schooners, are obviously exhilarated. Brilliant charges along like a freight train at better than nine knots, all plain sail flying, water creaming through the lee freeing ports as she lays the rail under, spray booming over the bows.

A Nantucket sleighride, indeed. In the days of whaling from open boats, a Nantucket sleighride often commenced the moment the harpooner in the whaleboat sank his iron into the whale. The startled whale might swim furiously for the horizon, dragging the boat at the end of its long tether. It was a wild ride, as the double-ended whaleboat surfed the wake of the Leviathan; at the finish of it, the spent whale was killed, or escaped into the deep, or stove the boat. This is not exactly that kind of sleighride, but it will do.

The foredeck is drenched and the next time I go onto the bow I wear my storm lowers, against the spray, and watch the whales playing all around us.

Later on, in early afternoon, we did reef. "This won't cut our speed, but it will balance the helm and reduce heel a little," Captain George explained. So we got a chance to reef down the main and made a fast neat job of it. Doug was clearly impressed.

We barreled along for hours under a blue sky, whales all around us. Soon we were off Nantucket Island, and the wind was dying out. We eked the last breath out of it, then all hands bent to sail drill. The fisherman came down first and we folded and bagged it on deck. I crawled out on the bowsprit and unhanked the lapper jib, passing it to Doug on the footropes who passed it to Mike to stuff into a sailbag and wrestle to its space below, behind the companionway ladder. So with the fisherman.

Next to be doused was the fores'l, its heavy top gaff lowered to the boom, the boom rested in a bronze socket against the mainmast, the whole sail then flaked and secured with sail ties between gaff and boom.

At last we lowered the giant mains'l for the first time since leaving Halifax. It slid down the tree gracefully, all hands standing by to fold it into a neat harbor furl. Like a coxswain, Doug called the cadence: "Ready—lift! Pull! Tuck!" It took only minutes. We were a crew.

Under Captain George's direction, I steered *Brilliant* into the channel in moderate traffic. I was not entirely comfortable maneuvering such a big vessel into a busy harbor, but I took my cue from George. "Left a bit," he would say, quietly. "Now right and hold it. Good. Leave that buoy fine to port. Stay near the lighthouse on shore. Right."

He took the wheel casually, held the kingspoke in his fingertips and stood to one side of the cockpit for an unobstructed view over the bow. Doug was on the radio asking about a mooring, but in the end we had to anchor with our own ground tackle.

George swung us easily alongside *Appledore*, a whale-watching schooner with a full crew lined at the rail waving to us, then headed *Brilliant* to an anchorage out in the harbor.

Doug and I unlashed the kedge anchor amidships and manhandled it to the foredeck, where we slipped the stock in place, locked it with a key-pin, and shackled it to the chain lead. Meanwhile Clint had unfastened the port-side foot ropes to allow the anchor a clear drop. At the order, we let it go and ran out two shots (at 15 fathoms a shot, that's 180 feet) of chain. George backed *Brilliant* down, away from the anchor till it set, then killed the engine.

For a moment we all just stood around on deck, listening to the silence, the strange hush of all motion stopped for the first time in three days. Then we resumed our chores.

7
★ ★ ★

Nantucket
to Vineyard Haven

At Nantucket we were without a tender. Stranded, as it were, in the open harbor, we were too far from shore to swim there, so we radioed the harbor launch to come out. We all spruced up and jumped aboard for the two-dollar ride—one way. It would cost two dollars apiece to get back.

Ordinarily *Brilliant* tows her own tender, *Afterglow*, a replica of a Herreshoff lifeboat. Captain George had left her in Mystic, since she could be swamped in ocean seas and therefore was not safe to tow astern, and was too big to carry on deck. Originally, *Brilliant* carried a nine-foot Nevins dinghy lashed amidships.

Afterglow is a nineteen-foot, graceful little craft which mimics *Brilliant*'s white topsides, accented by a green trunk stripe matching *Brilliant*'s boot top. *Afterglow* is painted in delicate gold letters across her varnished semi-wineglass transom. Naturally, *Afterglow* carries no engine, unless you count the "armstrong" engine: two pairs of oars set into oarlocks. Her inside is custard yellow and her seats are painted dado brown. According to the mate, it takes nearly two months of painting, varnishing, and general maintenance just to get *Afterglow* ready to go to sea each season.

Nantucket is no longer Melville's Nantucket, that hardy whaling port teeming with exotic men who made their living in the watery part of the world. Now the island is a yachting port and a tourist spot, full of well-to-do kids on summer break from college. Walking its narrow streets, you can't escape the impression that many of its shops are owned by newcomers, from Boston, New York, and elsewhere, who take eager advantage of Nantucket's checkered history. Like so many places of former character, it is feeding off its past, or more specifically, living off the most superficial and visual element of its past; marketing its own quaintness.

This is not a new phenomenon. The discovery of oil in Pennsylvania, the Civil War, and the increasing difficulty of getting the big whalers over the Nantucket Bar caused the island to turn to tourism by the 1870s—scarcely a generation and a half after Melville's *Pequod* sailed in quest of the white whale.

It is undeniably pleasant to walk around such a place, to feel the rough surface of cobbles underfoot instead of hard flat sidewalks, to watch horsedrawn carriages clatter by, to see so many people out walking on the street after dark. It is pleasant in the way it is pleasant to be anywhere that is full of people on vacation, people in no hurry, glad just to be there, spending money without counting it too closely.

And it has a terrific ice cream store, a good bookstore, and at least one cozy tavern where punchy sailors like us could sit and josh each other and talk over and over about the fog, the big wind that had brought us here, the sleighride, the ship that, literally, passed in the night, the long night watches, the thrill in the stomach as *Brilliant* spanked along dipping her lee rail, and the whales.

However much Nantucket had bartered its heritage to serve the tourists, it was still, as it had been since before Melville, a place of whales. We had seen whales. And we had seen them without the obligation of hunting them down, without the slaughter and industry of the whaler's bloody cutting stage and oily, smoking tryworks.

So not all change had been for the worse. Something crucial had been saved, after all. And though some tourists come for the shops, for the illusion of nineteenth century quaintness, for the yacht parties, what many really come for still, I think, are the whales.

Probably, I realize now, I was unfair to Nantucket. Very likely, my strong adverse reaction to Nantucket was due in part to the illusion it spoiled for me—the illusion of my own adventure aboard *Brilliant*. At sea, for three days in fog and wind and weather, engine and radar or no, it had been possible to believe that we were somehow sharing in the heritage of those men, long dead now, who had gone to sea at risk of life and limb. Melville's Nantucketer who, out of sight of land, "lays him to his rest while under his very pillow rush herds of walruses and whales."

But we had not, exactly. We had voyaged in relative safety; we had not gone down into the Southern Ocean or around the Cape of Storms or into the icepack of Greenland. We had only come a short way, down a known coast, with every aid to navigation the twentieth century could provide, with hot food and warm bunks, in a vessel that was in every way at the top of her class.

How could what we had done compare with real seafaring?

It could only give us a taste, the merest shadow of the danger those old sailing ships must have faced on every voyage, the smallest inkling of their hardship, the tiniest glimmer of insight about their courage and resourcefulness.

Back aboard, sleep came easily, the gentle harbor swell just enough to rock me into dreaming. Captain George had already announced that we could sleep in. We could make Martha's Vineyard easily in a few hours' sail, so there was no pressing need to rise and get underway early.

Nevertheless, by eight o'clock I was up, feeling rested and alert, and joined Dean and Clint on deck. Both were just toweling down from a swim in the harbor. The kids were still snug in their bunks. There was a slight breeze, a little overcast. The water looked gray and cold.

"Really, it's not too bad," Clint said. Dean was combing out his long hair and then rebraiding it. "Give it a try," Clint said.

"How deep is the water here?" I asked.

"Fifteen, maybe twenty feet," Clint said. "You can dive."

Dean (left) and Clint.
(Author's photo)

"How do I get back aboard?"

"Climb up the bobstay and the footropes."

So I shallow-dived off the bow and swam for a few minutes in that cold water. After the initial shock, it was exhilarating. I swam under the bow and grabbed onto the bobstay, the cable that runs from the waterline at the bow to the end of the bowsprit, compensating for the load put on the bowsprit by the jibstay. I hauled myself up and grabbed the footropes, swung my feet up into their net and in a jiffy was back aboard, towel around my shoulders, watching the early ferry come across the channel to dock at Nantucket.

I was to go back over the side before long.

Brilliant's topsides—the outer hull from waterline to bulwarks—are a gleaming white. They are so white that, if you photograph them, as I did, they reflect back to the camera the ripply water, the dock, the photographer. Like a mirror, or clean glass. A photo of the topsides resembles the reflection in a still pond. Keeping those topsides so bright is a constant and difficult job. Repainting the topsides—the exacting job entrusted to the Essex Boat Works in Essex, Connecticut, where *Brilliant* visits every April—is an $8,000 proposition, so it pays to protect the current high-gloss finish.

One phenomenon that can mar the topsides finish is collision—with a dock, another vessel, a tender, flotsam at sea—so large soft-plastic fenders sheathed in terrycloth are used to cushion the hull from the sharp edges of a wooden pier, or a launch bobbing in a choppy swell.

A more common problem is that bronze railtop fittings—lifeline stanchions and shroud turnbuckles in particular—tend to "bleed" down onto the white topsides. Periodically those thin brown trails must be scrubbed off.

Today I volunteered to begin the job. I put on gym shorts and my reefer and was lowered over the side in the bosun's chair, which was shackled to the main halyard. Clint and Dean did the heave-ho-ing. My legs, from the knees down, dangled in the water. Using Nevrdull, a kind of stiff batting saturated with brass polish, I scrubbed off line after line, first on the starboard side, then on the port.

While I was busy in the bosun's chair, the rest of the crew polished brass, aired bedding, and in general tidied up the ship. At sea, with navigation and sailhandling to keep us busy, we had gotten a little sloppy. Now was the time to put the ship back in order, which included unrigging and stowing the jacklines.

After a breakfast of french toast and coffee, George spread out the charts in the cockpit and laid out our choices: We could continue west along the south side of the Sound to Martha's Vineyard, putting in at Edgartown or Vineyard Haven; or we could try to make Newport or Block Island in one long hop. Since we had another whole day to make either of the latter before sailing easily on to Mystic, we voted for Martha's Vineyard.

I had my own reason for wanting to go to that island: Joshua Slocum's home was there, still standing in West Tisbury, looking by all accounts just the way it had when the old sailor had left it four generations ago.

At 1045 we winched up the anchor, Mike and I doubling up on the windlass while Doug hosed the mud off the chain and anchor as they came aboard. Then we lashed the anchor in the foot ropes to be handy in case we had to anchor at Vineyard Haven.

Even as we were lashing the anchor, the remainder of both watches were bending to sail drill, hauling up the main and then, for the first time on the passage, bending on the gollywobbler—a lightweight oversized version of the fisherman stays'l that flies between foremast and mainmast, stretching peak to peak and down nearly to the deck, all 1,200 square feet of it. We added another 900 feet at the bowsprit—the ballooner jib—and went busting out of the harbor under sail, pushing nine knots, and flying 3,075 square feet of canvas.

Nantucket and Coatue Point fell off on our port quarter, then Eel Point, the westernmost headland of Nantucket Island, and Tuckernuck Island came onto our beam and then Muskeget Island, and finally the infamous Chappaquiddick Island.

Watches were called off—we would be daysailing from now on. We crossed the Muskeget Channel with a sharp lookout for lobster pots, usually laid out in lines of half a dozen or more, white or red floats protruding vertical sticks. Sometimes we slalomed among whole fields of them. Trawlers were all over the place, some of them steaming so slowly that they were obviously dragging nets.

But it was much like the sailing we had done yesterday as we had come spanking into the mouth of Nantucket Sound past the upper fang of Monomoy Island on the Cape Cod side and the lower fang of Great Point, Nantucket. Now visibility was virtually unlimited, though the blue sky was dirty with overcast that blew away on the steady Northeast wind as the day wore on. We wore shorts and t-shirts on deck—summer clothes. The foul weather gear stayed in the lockers below. We headed northeast by west and then northwest to follow the northward curve of Martha's Vineyard, past Oak Bluffs, and finally to Vineyard Haven harbor.

This time the wind did not slacken. We had 20 knots across Muskeget Channel and about 15 knots coming into harbor in a light drizzle. We close-reached in and struck sails once inside the harbor. It was a quick, efficient sail drill—it had to be. Every mooring was occupied, and plenty of craft of all sizes rode at anchor close to shore.

At the harbormaster's instruction, we came alongside *Zorro*, a ketch as large as *Brilliant*, and rafted there for the night. The passage had taken only a little more than five hours, anchor to mooring.

From my log:

> We are in distinguished company. Just offshore is moored the old pilot schooner Alabama, *now being refitted. The transom has been opened up, and new wood shows in the gash, covered by canvas, like a wound healing. Off our port quarter rides* Moxie, *the sleek white trimaran designed for the late Philip Weld and which he sailed to record-breaking victory in the 1980 Observer Singlehanded Transatlantic Race (OSTAR).*
>
> *And somewhere in this little harbor rides the ghost of Joshua Slocum's little oyster sloop* Spray. *She did not have* Brilliant's *graceful lines; she had a broad deck, a full bow, a narrow transom stern cut off short, and no engine but her sails and a pair of stout oars.*
>
> *Still, he took her around the world, and we have come only from Halifax, not far from the old captain's childhood home on the Bay of Fundy.*
>
> *He would approve, though, of bringing a wooden ship into harbor under sail. He would admire our smart sail drill.*

8

★ ★ ★

Vineyard Haven to Block Island

Martha's Vineyard, like our other ports of call on this passage, is still easier to reach by boat than by automobile—quite a claim in this day of interstate highways and car phones. The ferry from Cape Cod is booked solid all summer long, and one must make arrangements far in advance to assure a place.

The harbor at Vineyard Haven, formerly "Holmes Hole," was smaller than the one at Nantucket and, for other reasons as well, cozier. Though the whole island has long since been given over to tourists, somehow it has retained an essential maritime character. Two hundred yards from our mooring, for instance, Nat Benjamin's boatyard was spread along the beach. Nat builds and repairs wooden boats. One of his gaff-headed sloops, recently commissioned, rode at the wharf that juts out in front of his place. Among the many fiberglass boats, big molded plastic toys, she stood out in the soft-spoken but insistent way of new wood bent into fair lines, of a hand-worked sheer curve mirrored on bright water.

The yard was headquartered in an old shed, plywood-patched and tar-papered and shored up with scrap framing, its dirt floor littered with tools and chunks of exotic wood. On the ways outside were drawn up two large sailboats, full-keel jobs draped with tarpaulins, surrounded by scaffolding, as Nat and his people worked on them with all the attention of surgeons, in no particular hurry, fitting wood precisely.

On the harbor beach were stranded half a dozen sailing dinghies and rowboats, along with knocked-down cradle beams, pipes, scaffolding, and other debris incident to building boats. When some of our crew first came ashore on the harbor launch (this one cost only $1), Clint and Dean were naturally drawn to the boatyard. I tagged along and stood in the shadow of an ocean-going ketch whose stem was being replaced while they searched out Ginny Jones, now an employee of Nat's, whom they had known at Mystic.

Ginny Jones, a robust woman who has been around ships and boats all her adult life, produced two cars about the time the harbor launch produced Captain George and the rest of our crew (except Doug, who remained on board, and Dave, who went off to look up an old friend), and we set out for her home in Tisbury. Clint had supervised the off-loading of grocery bags full of supper supplies, and the plan was to cook at Ginny Jones' house in a real kitchen.

On the way we made a brief detour to West Tisbury and stopped in front of the old farmhouse once owned by Joshua Slocum. It was bare white clapboard, unadorned and very Yankee looking, identified by a small marker at the edge of the property. It was still a private residence, though it was no longer as isolated as it must have been in Captain Slocum's heyday. He had bought it for his second wife, Hettie, with the dubious ambition of settling into the life of a farmer. He put in an orchard and made small improvements to the house and property—fences, shutters, a shake shingle roof that he ferried over in bundles from the mainland on his *Spray*, as precious a cargo as the old sloop ever carried. He roofed the house himself, but after that mostly lived on his boat, in one port or another, visiting Tisbury from time to time but rarely for long, until his final voyage.

It was exactly what I had expected, and yet not at all what I had expected. I had known of Slocum all this time as a legend, a man whose adventures had been exaggerated to heroism, to myth almost, and it was an unexpected shock to have that man so suddenly reduced to mere human stature. He had lived in a small, unexceptional house, on a little piece of land, on a pictures-que island. I could imagine him there during those short-lived days while he busied himself in the unlikely role of planter and husband, peeking out from behind the window to size up his visitors and decide whether to offer them a glass of cider. He was a man, they say, who loved having visitors, loved it that people sought him out to hear him tell seafaring stories, watch him work and sail. He would brew them up a fish chowder of his own recipe on the kit-chen stove, though he was evidently more accustomed to the open brazier on *Spray*'s deck.

He had sailed off, from the very harbor where *Brilliant* now rode at mooring, seventy-eight years ago, never to be heard from again. I had always imagined him just sailing on and on, a sort of Flying Yankee on the seas of the world. But not, as with the Dutchman and his diabolical crew, living out an eternal penance for the sin of blasphemy; rather, as a kind of reward, the unique privilege of sailing through a heaven under his keel, world without end: the only kind of heaven he would have wanted.

Now, seeing that little plain house, imagining the old bald-headed, pointy-bearded captain once alive there, it was possible to imagine him dead —the victim of accident or neglect or weather. A steamship had run him down in the night in the Hatteras lanes, his son Victor had always maintained; others, that finally his seamanship had failed, or *Spray*'s too-light rigging, or that he had been overwhelmed in a line squall.

We drove away. Ginny Jones had the excellent good grace to slap cold bottles of Molson's Ale in our hands (soft drinks for the kids) when we reached her house, and she and Clint set to work concocting a monumental spaghetti dinner, complete with garlic bread, spicy sauce, and a salad that would have been a meal unto itself.

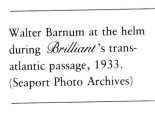

Walter Barnum at the helm during *Brilliant*'s trans-atlantic passage, 1933. (Seaport Photo Archives)

After supper, she showed us some photographic prints she had acquired in England: *Brilliant* as done by Beken of Cowes, Ltd., the premier maritime photographers in Britain since the 1880s. The photos depicted *Brilliant* with her old gaff-headed mains'l, Walter Barnum at the helm, racing sometime in the 1930s.

Those photos recalled for me the film footage that had been shot during *Brilliant*'s record transatlantic crossing in 1933, which I had first seen as part of a video presentation at Mystic Seaport Museum and which I have watched many times since. The footage is remarkable to me for its quality and for the sense it conveys of the past, of dynamic memory faded to black and white: bearish Walter Barnum in wire-rimmed glasses, porkpie hat, and polka-dot tie, grinning for the camera; spray crashing over the bows, the lee deck awash; young bearded sailors sporting dark crew neck sweaters and yachting caps, dangling cigarettes off their lips Bogart-style or puffing pipes.

Watching the film, I watched a ghost, I thought, an artifact from another era, like those flickering Vitagraph images of the Rough Riders' charge up San Juan Hill, of men now dead and machines dismantled and places long gone.

But this *Brilliant* was the same one I was sailing. She even looked about the same, if you jibbed the main and put Clint and Dean and Doug on the foredeck instead of those anonymous hired sailors of Barnum's. She had sailed through a long stint of history, even across the great watershed of the Second World War, intact and working. Amazing.

Even her name, *Brilliant*, has a provenance of sorts: the original *Brilliant* was a British wool clipper in the Australian trade, a square-rigger, discovered by Barnum in an old photograph of Sydney harbor.

Our evening ashore was to be capped by a visit to David's Island House at the invitation of our absent crew member, Dave. So we piled into the cars once again and headed for Oak Bluffs on the eastern shore of the Vineyard. Oak Bluffs was the site of the original tourist settlement on the Vineyard —a Methodist camp meeting started in 1835.

With a little luck parking in that crowded and boisterous town, which now resembles anything but a church camp, we were soon comfortably arranged around a large table sipping cocktails and soft drinks, courtesy of Dave.

David, who owned the place and was the old friend Dave had been seeking, turned out to be a blind piano player of exceptional style. We listened to his jazzy music, toasted the ship and each other and David and Dave, and by midnight were back on the launch, slicing the still water of the harbor toward our ship. The sky was full of unrealized cumulus. The short-lived afternoon drizzle was the only rain we'd have tonight, but I was glad enough to have carried ashore my reefer, for the air had turned chill. I put it on and turned up the collar against the damp. We were still tired, the kind of tired that gets into your bones and takes more than one night's sleep to satisfy.

Tomorrow would be an early day and a long sail, and we were getting close enough to home to be missing our ship, and our shipmates, already.

We cast off mooring lines at 0730, before breakfast, into a steady north wind of about 10 knots and a fair current. After beating out of the harbor, we settled down for a fast reach down the length of Vineyard Sound, that channel separating the northwest shore of Martha's Vineyard from the Elizabeth Islands. Flying gollywobbler, ballooner, and main, we passed them one by one off to starboard and reeled off their Indian names, all that remains of their original inhabitants: Naushon, Pasque, Nashawena, and Cuttyhunk, doing better than 10 knots over the bottom and following a rhumb line for Block Island.

Vineyard Sound was full of lobster pots and fishing boats, and we maneuvered close around these obstacles. We were practiced at helmsmanship by now. The cross seas made the helm tricky as we passed Cuttyhunk and spied the flashing Buzzard's Bay Light, a bright red tower on a steel chassis protruding from the water. Buzzard's Bay lies on the northwest side of the Elizabeth Islands, and at the light it and Vineyard Sound run into Rhode Island Sound.

Now we were in open water again, still reaching handily on the north wind. Miles off to port lay the only other land between us and Block Island, a little island at the outer edge of a shoal, called, ominously, No Man's Land.

The word "schooner" derives, tradition and Webster maintain, from a Scots dialect Yankee word, variously written "scun" or "scoon," meaning "to skim or skip upon the water." Although the rig it describes is a century older, the earliest traceable use of the word was early in the eighteenth century around Gloucester, Massachusetts, later renowned for its fleet of fishing schooners. The *Oxford English Dictionary* cites an apocryphal tale of a Yankee ship-launching: as the first of this new breed of fore-and-after slid down the ways, a spectator was reported to have said, "Oh, how she scoons!" To which Captain Andrew Robinson, the builder, replied, "A schooner let her be!"

That's exactly what we were doing, *schooning. Brilliant* belonged as much to the air as to the sea as she leapt from wave top to wave top, streaming a trail of creamy foam. The seas were running only about two feet or so. The sky was clear and cloudless.

By 1000 the wind had veered enough to make the gollywobbler, a reaching sail, inefficient, so we struck it and bent on the fisherman, raising that and the fores'l for windward work.

We snacked on sandwiches and fruit and polished all the brass, then settled in for the ride. We took turns at the helm as *Brilliant* beat across the mouth of Narragansett Bay and beyond Point Judith.

Now well into Block Island Sound, we made Sandy Point, Block Island, off to port, then fell off the wind to head south into New Harbor, which opens off the island's northwest shore. As usual, we charged in under canvas and only struck sail in the inner harbor.

The mate was already fond of telling us we were his best crew of the season, and we were all, I think, aware that we were playing to an audience. When *Brilliant* enters a harbor heads turn, motor yachts chug closer for a better look, and small boat sailors stare and nod as if a smartly-crewed schooner under full sail is the right answer to an important question they have been asking all their lives.

So you try to do things right the first time. You listen hard for the captain's quiet orders. You try to be in the right place even before you are told to be there. You watch for out-of-place gear and stow it without a remark. You look around for chores that need doing, shipmates who need a hand. And you do all this more or less instinctively. Your bones know you depend on each other and on the ship; your hands start to think for themselves.

Sails furled, we motored through the moorings of the congested harbor, Captain George now at the helm and looking very tropical in his canvas-brimmed sailing hat and dark glasses. He edged *Brilliant* close to the long main dock of Block Island Boat Basin and then backed the engine and shifted it to neutral gear, so that we stopped neatly within hailing distance of the dockmaster's shack.

One berth at the inboard end of the pier was still vacant, and it was to be ours. After some thought, George motored along the pier and swung the bow away from it. That done, he ordered a kedge set from the port bow. Clint, Doug, and I shackled on the Danforth anchor and lowered away on command, and Captain George slowly backed *Brilliant* down on it and into the slip. Dean leaped ashore and, with help from the dockmaster, secured a stern line. The rest of the crew now handled mooring lines, and within a few minutes *Brilliant* was snug in her berth, transom held safely off the pier, spring lines hitched to the pilings, kedge snubbed taut.

It was a neat bit of seamanship. That Captain George did it in such a seemingly offhand manner was all the more remarkable. Sailboats, as a rule, do not maneuver well in close quarters under power. They are unresponsive and back down poorly, and *Brilliant* was no exception. Nevertheless, she had just backed into a narrow slip in a crowded harbor on the first try.

As our bowsprit and a good fifteen feet of our bow protruded into the channel, and since we had set an anchor even farther off than that, Captain George ordered a riding light set on the end of the bowsprit for the night—to ward off any careless hot-rodders in motorized zodiac boats.

Tonight we would have hot showers and the convenience of coming and going just by stepping off onto the dock. But first came the vessel. Not since Halifax had we had access to a freshwater hose, and George meant to take full advantage of it. At his direction, I sprayed down the topsides port and starboard, then, beginning at the bow, rinsed the deck and brightwork. The whole crew followed along behind, chamois in hand, wiping madly, until all the wood was clean of salt.

Next, of course, we polished all the brass, and laid out sheets to dry. Doug went to work on the topsides as I had in Nantucket, scrubbing off the brown streaks that had bled from the bronze lifeline stanchions. The heads were cleaned and below decks aired and straightened, and we were free to go ashore. Dinner would be served on board at seven: chili, cornbread, and the last of our chocolate chip cookies, which Clint had been hoarding for one last dessert.

On the hill overlooking the Block Island marina is a bar and restaurant, built over top of a clean and spacious shower block. Clint, Doug, Dean, Captain George, and I took advantage of a shower and fresh clothes, then climbed up onto the large wrap-around wooden porch of the bar and drank rum and beer with the curious perspective of a West Coaster: we watched the sun go down over water. The air turned chilly, as we talked about what we always talked about together—boats and sailing—and watched some lucky fishermen unload three gigantic tunas from the ice-hold of their boat and carry them, with some effort, down the pier to the back of a station wagon.

Our faces were sunburned and windchapped, and we all felt relaxed. Tomorrow we would be home, and it had been a good passage. The ship was safely bedded down for the night, and the drinks had mellowed us and put an edge on our hunger. So after awhile we walked down the hill and back down the dock toward *Brilliant*, passing along the way a dozen or so cocktail parties on the backporch decks of monstrous power boats—what sailors call "stinkpots."

Some of the boaters lined along that dock, stern-to, never go anywhere, Captain George explained. They keep their boats here like second homes and use them for weekend parties.

Next to our slip was berthed a center-cockpit sloop, forty-five feet or so. Two ladies relaxed in the cockpit under an awning. A little dog—a fuzzy lhasa apsa—was harnessed and tied so that he could roam the deck. His harness had a handle at the top, like a suitcase, presumably so the dog could be picked up and carried without fuss: portable dog. When he wandered too far, however, one of the ladies casually wrapped his leash around the genoa winch and hauled him in, the winch clacketing and the miniature dog backpedaling on the slippery fiberglass deck for all he was worth. We found this hilarious.

"Sheet in the dog!" Clint said, and we liked it so much we said it over and over that night and laughed everytime we heard it.

9
★ ★ ★

Block Island
to Mystic

In the morning we retrieved the kedge as smartly as we had set it. The day was coming up fine and clear with a steady West by North breeze. Clint hosed off the chain as we winched it clear of the water and we catted the Danforth on the port whisker strut to leave all hands free to handle sails. Meanwhile, stern lines were eased and cast off, spring lines taken aboard, and Captain George motored us gently away from the dock.

We busted out of New Harbor close-hauled and flying all plain sail, including the ballooner. *Brilliant* heeled into her track, moving so fast Captain George had to crack the sheets to slow her down and avoid running up the transoms of two big power yachts chugging outbound side by side, barely making headway and blocking the whole channel. George gave them a friendly blast on the portable canned horn, but it took two more before the sociable skippers ahead of us woke up and realized they were blocking navigation in the heavy channel traffic.

We cranked in the sheets and flew by them to open water.

As soon as we were clear of the channel, George asked if any of the crew would like to take the wheel. I jumped at the chance, knowing it might be a long spell before I had a forty-two-ton schooner under me again. The kids really seemed played out, content to laze in the sun tanning their necks and faces and legs. We still wore long-sleeved shirts. They stretched out along the side decks and closed their eyes against the sun and enjoyed the ride.

Last night we had all lingered at the main saloon table after supper, rested and full. Someone suggested a game of Trivial Pursuit. We played teams: Michelle, Doug, Mike, and I against Liesel, Dean, John, and Clint. Captain George had changed into fresh shore clothes but stayed around to watch the game. We cleaned their clocks, but the main thing was the sense of solidarity, the spirit of the thing, the easy laughter and good natured teasing from all quarters.

The kids had joshed us about getting them a sixpack of beer when we went ashore. We didn't of course, but it seemed ironic that the same teenager who had rolled out of a warm bunk at 4:00 A.M., with benefit of only four hours of sleep after a five-hour watch, to don storm gear and crawl out onto

a dark and slippery deck in raw cold and fog a hundred miles out into the Atlantic, then take the helm of a sixty-two-foot schooner and carry the lives of nine other people on his nerve, concentration, and stamina, should be too young to have a legal bottle of beer ashore.

Clint smoked and Dean rode the bowsprit and even Captain George relaxed and smiled, perched on the lee cockpit coaming. After seven years, it was apparent that he still had a love affair going with *Brilliant*.

For me this was the final leg of a week's sailing, more or less, tacked onto two days of air travel and waiting at the dock in Halifax. But it finally occurred to me that Captain George, Doug, Clint, and Dean had been onboard for almost three weeks, sailing the Marblehead to Halifax race, taking on a new crew and making ready for sea, and then sailing back the way they had come. Dean missed his wife and Doug his fiancee. Now we were within an easy sail from home, their spirits were high.

In the adventure of the moment, the secret swift nighttime passage through fog or the spanking sleighride of a windy Nantucket Sound afternoon, it had been easy to forget just how much responsibility rides on the shoulders of captain and mate, even on a relatively small vessel such as *Brilliant*. But Captain George had taken our lives in his hands, had, with Doug's assistance, taken us offshore and taught us how to handle a sailing vessel with competence if not mastery.

69

The author at the helm.
(Author's photo)

Captain George held a 100-ton ocean operator's certificate from the U.S. Coast Guard, entitling him to the privilege and legal responsibility of our safety. Doug held a 100-ton coastal certificate. Both men were certified reliable sailors by the Coast Guard, yet every passage is a new passage, and even familiar waters change with the season, the day, the hour. Wind changes the terrain of the waves; fog wipes out landmarks; darkness obscures even obvious harbor entrances.

No sailor, no ship's captain, can ever afford to take for granted that this passage will be like the last. The sea, the weather are variable. So he must build on what he knows: his own seamanship and experience, the seaworthiness of the vessel under him, the reliability of his mate and crew, the tide tables, the compass, and the charts.

Brilliant was snoring along now, heeled far enough to dip her lee rail from time to time. The bows were wet from spray. "We could reef," George said with a sly smile, "but let's just enjoy this for awhile."

I held the wheel all the way to the Mystic River for two reasons. First, to take the helm of a big boat under sail in a brisk wind is just plain fun. You ride the roller-coaster waves, hear the spray boom across the bulwarks, and control it all with a light fingertip touch. Through your fingers, gentle on the

70

spoke, is transmitted the whole power of the hull and rig. All of it answers to your hand, and quickly. There is nothing else like it. Second, I felt I had not learned to steer nearly well enough. I often oversteered, compensating by oversteering in the opposite direction, and so on.

Captain George gave me a lesson in helmsmanship. "You're oversteering because you're not anticipating." he said. "Watch the bow come off the wave. The wave is pushing the bow away from your course. As the bow starts to slide down the wave, bring her up a spoke. As soon as she's down again, bring her back. You never have to give her more than a spoke either way."

Brilliant , with her marconi mainsail, takes a puff, 1988. (Photo by Mary Anne Stets)

72

He was right. There was a knack to it, but the key was paying attention to which way the waves hit the bow. Simple. After a few minutes, I could hold her on course virtually without correction.

George also advised me, in daylight coasting, to steer by the horizon instead of strictly by the compass: "Once you're on course, look over the bow and find a landmark. Steer for that. Every now and then, check to make sure you're more or less on your compass course, but you'll find it's easier to steer by the horizon."

Right again. After a couple of hours of practice, through sea changes and switches of current and point of sail, I was getting it. My most satisfying accomplishment of the passage was learning to steer *Brilliant* by the look and feel of the seas on her bow toward a landmark on the horizon.

In the early afternoon, Clint went aloft—scrambling right up the starboard shroud all the way to the crosstrees. The vessel was heeled better than 20 degrees, which made it, I imagine, somewhat easier on his balance. Around his neck dangled my camera, and when he had made sure of his balance, arm looped around the shroud, he focused it and shot the deck with its pinstriping of seams, the wet curve of the bows, the bright roiling sea, the cockpit starred in the center by the gold hexagon of the compass binnacle. Then he lowered the camera on the flag halyard.

Captain George said, "When you look at pictures taken from aloft, you'll be amazed at how narrow *Brilliant* is compared to today's ocean yachts. Especially lightweight racers, IOR, that kind. They have much greater beam."

True enough. It is almost disconcerting how narrow *Brilliant* is for her length, an old-fashioned engineering aesthetic in an age of sharp-bowed boats that belly out like teardrops just aft of amidships. In a hull, interior space increases faster as a function of beam than of length, so that a short broad hull will often be roomier belowdecks than a long slim one. A beamy hull is usually more stable than a narrow one, and will ride over the seas or even plane rather than cut through the seas. The genius of *Brilliant*'s design was that the narrow hull worked: she is a comfortable, seaworthy boat, though admittedly wet by modern standards.

By noon we were across Block Island Sound and in sight of Watch Hill, at the edge of a little finger of Rhode Island that juts down at the border of Connecticut. To port stood Fisher's Island, New York. We were in home waters, schooning along in 15 knots of breeze, surrounded by hundreds of sailboats and powerboats and lobsterpots and fishermen, slaloming and occasionally tacking toward free water. Captain George often took the helm now for tricky maneuvering and all hands were busy easing and hardening sheets, manning the backstays, keeping lookout.

We spied *Mystic Clipper* and *Voyager*, two schooners of the Mystic windjammer fleet, outbound.

As we entered the Mystic River, really a long narrow tidal wash, the inevitable order came: strike all sails. Our drill was just as fast and smart as ever, but I felt a real pang as I helped haul down the main and flake it over the boom, then tie it off with sail-ties and cradle the boom. Our sail was over. The diesel revved and Captain George piloted us upriver.

73

Looking aloft.
(Author's photo)

Coming up on the Mystic drawbridge, Captain George treated us to one last lesson in boathandling. The drawbridge opens at a quarter past the hour, the opening preceded by a bell and then a siren. George calculated *Brilliant*'s speed up the river so that she would reach the bridge just as it opened. Our way was blocked by a fleet of miscellaneous boats—everything from sailing dinghies to bluewater motor yachts, many of them skippered by people who obviously did not know what they were doing. They milled around, tacking and backing and generally confusing the channel. Captain George threaded *Brilliant* through the motley fleet and up to the bridge at precisely the moment when the siren sounded and the great steel jaw of the bridge lifted with the movement of the big fist-shaped counterweight.

Brilliant slid under straight and easy, center channel, with the fleet maneuvering to catch up.

We slipped past the Gloucester fishing schooner *L.A. Dunton* and the steam-powered ferry *Sabino* to the point of the Mystic Seaport promontory, marked by a lighthouse. On the other side were berthed the whaling bark *Charles W. Morgan,* and the iron, square-rigged former training ship *Joseph Conrad.* Captain George brought her around, neutralized the engine, and let the wind drift *Brilliant* down on her wharf softly as a kiss.

From my log:

Mystic Pier. We spent three hours hosing down and wiping topsides and deck. Even the spars needed washing down, as they had been sprayed constantly with saltwater on our passage from Block Island, We shined the brightwork and polished all the brass on deck and belowdecks—including ports, instruments, plaques, locker fittings, and anything else meant to gleam.

Doug, Dean, and I fitted on sailcovers to match the sandy wheel and binnacle covers, then I went below to scrub out the aft and midships heads. Meanwhile, others scoured the cabin sole and squeegied dry the whole ship from fo'c'sle to companionway. We pumped out the bilge and opened all ports and skylights to vent ship.

One by one, we hoisted out our duffels and lugged them ashore to the long white shop that is Brilliant's Mystic Seaport headquarters. We lingered in the cockpit eating sandwiches and the last of the apples and drinking fresh iced tea.

One by one, each of the crew signed the guest book, shook hands all round, and said goodbye. At the parting, Captain George gave each a swallow-tailed blue-and-red Brilliant emblem—a miniature pennant to sew onto a favorite hat or shirt.

At last only Captain George and I were left and there seemed nothing else that needed doing onboard. As we walked away from Brilliant, George noticed a sloppy dockline and stepped back aboard to coil it properly. I climbed aboard behind him to reattach two shackles securing the footropes at the bowsprit, which we had unfastened to swing the anchor back aboard and lash it onto its proper chocks amidships.

We took a last look. Brilliant fairly sparkled. We smiled and walked away.

It was clear that none of us wanted to leave the ship. In some measure, I suppose, that speaks for the success of the passage—that we should feel such reluctance and regret at the prospect of resuming a life of hot food served on a level table, stationary bunks with fresh bedding, regular showers, privacy, sleeping the night through without being called on deck in the bone-chilling fog, clean clothes, and no brass to polish.

But I know my regret was real, partly, I guess, because this had been my first passage on a tall ship, and my first offshore passage as well. And there is never any thrill exactly like the first.

I had learned some things: how to steer a compass course, then how to steer by the horizon; how to tie a slippery reef knot in the dark; how to set a gaff-rigged sail (throat first, then peak); how to overhaul a line safely and effectively (never between block and winch); how to climb out onto a "widowmaker" and work there comfortably; how to set a fisherman stays'l and a gollywobbler; how the Swedish watch system, in practice, works; how Loran works; how to read a radar scope and use it to alter course; how to throw a tugboat hitch on a mooring bit; how to properly clear, coil, and hang sheets and halyards; how to fold sails neatly on a pitching deck; how to properly furl a sail on a boom; how to steer a good course in a cross sea; the satisfying sense of cooperation when it matters, when safety is at stake; being part of a crew and looking out for the ship; how it feels to be out on deep water in a big sailing ship.

Before her next trip, *Brilliant* will be reprovisioned. Captain and mate will tinker with gear, adjust the radar, check the ship from stem to stern. By the end of October, she will be warped to the Mystic dock for the winter—her masts unstepped by crane and put in covered storage at Rossie Mill. During the cold idle months, volunteers, some of them local college students, will work with George and Doug at maintenance—cleaning, refinishing cabinets, painting overheads, polishing, tuning, repairing. *Brilliant*'s $15,000 annual maintenance budget does not cover salaries.

When she's back from Essex in April, they'll restep her masts, rig her, and start another season under sail.

The old stories: a stranger comes to town, or someone goes on a journey.

There is one more story: the homecoming.

The voyage ends, the sailor comes back from the sea and stretches his land legs under him, walks up the hill, and goes home. And for the first few hours ashore, the first wobbly days, and on still nights for a long time after, as winter winds freeze the high stars and snow muffles the pounding of breakers against sand, he closes his eyes and feels the sway of the deck in his legs, in the bones of his ears. Even faraway, his body remembers: the earth is mostly water. He lies awake and listens, dreaming of blue water, full sails, a fast ship, a brilliant passage.

Appendix

Brilliant's Racing Career

After building *Brilliant*, Walter Barnum became an avid yachtsman. He joined the New York Yacht Club, the Cruising Club of America, and Britain's Royal Ocean Yacht Club. After sailing her to a sixth-place finish in the 1932 Bermuda Race, Barnum took *Brilliant* to England in 1933. Her near-record transatlantic passage preceded a disappointing fourth-place finish in the Fastnet Race. *Brilliant* again sailed in the Bermuda Race in 1936, finishing second. A decade later, in her last ocean race before coming to Mystic, she finished tenth in the Bermuda Race. Owner Briggs Cunningham realized that she had become outclassed as design rules changed, and he did not race her again offshore.

Brilliant's 1932 Bermuda Race crew. They are (left to right) the paid cook and his assistant, Joe Appleton, Fred Bradley, Alf Loomis (the yachting writer who served as navigator for the race), Graham Bigelow, Lank Ford, owner Walter Barnum at the wheel behind an unidentified crewmember, Burral Barnum, and a paid hand. (Rosenfeld Collection, Mystic Seaport Museum.)

Captain George Moffett
(right) and Mate Jeff Stone,
with trophies won by
Brilliant in 1985. (Photo by
Mary Anne Stets)

Since her donation to the Mystic Seaport Museum by Briggs Cunningham in 1953, *Brilliant* has raced in local and coastal regattas, though no records are available to indicate either her success or her general performance.

Captain Bowker added other races to *Brilliant*'s schedule in the 1970s, including The Classic Yacht Regatta in Newport, Rhode Island, and The Traditional Boat Weekend (now known as the Governor's Cup) of Essex, Connecticut.

In 1986 and 1987, Captain Moffett entered *Brilliant* in The Opera House Cup of Nantucket, finishing first and second, respectively, in the fleet of more than 50 boats; in 1985 and 1986 she raced for The Mayor's Cup of New York City and on both occasions was first to finish and second on corrected time.

Captain Moffett offers the following account of his racing experience aboard *Brilliant*:

"Also in '86 we entered the first ocean race for *Brilliant* since her participation in the 1946 Bermuda Race. In this case we raced from Boston to Cape

Sable, Nova Scotia, in 1986 and Marblehead to Halifax in 1987. The latter event is regarded as a major ocean race, whereas the former (1986) was a minor event organized for schooners from the U.S. and Nova Scotia. She finished first (elapsed time) over the line in the schooners event of '86, having averaged nine knots for the 245-mile course. She did not do well in the light air race of '87 to Halifax.

"This summary may be useful:

	1985	1986	1987
Nantucket Opera House Cup	——	1st (fleet)	2nd (fleet
Classic Yacht Regatta, Newport	1st (class)	1st (class)	1st (class)
Mystic Schooner Race	2nd	1st	DNF
Governor's Cup (Essex Traditional Boat Weekend)	2nd	1st	1st
Mayor's Cup of New York	2nd (corr.)*	2nd (corr.)*	—

*first to finish

"These are corrected time (handicapped) results. *Brilliant* also won the series trophy for best performance in three out of four races (Nantucket, Newport, Mystic, New York races) sponsored in 1985 by Foster's Lager and in 1986 by Mount Gay."

Ordinarily, *Brilliant* races with a teenage crew, on board for sail training, who learn to handle the boat during the course of the regatta.

★ ★ ★

Start of *Brilliant*'s first ocean race, the 1932 Bermuda Race. *Brilliant* is flanked by *Highland Light* (left) and *Sea Witch*. (M.S.M. 65.343.35)

These two profiles illustrate
the change from gaff to
marconi rig on the main.

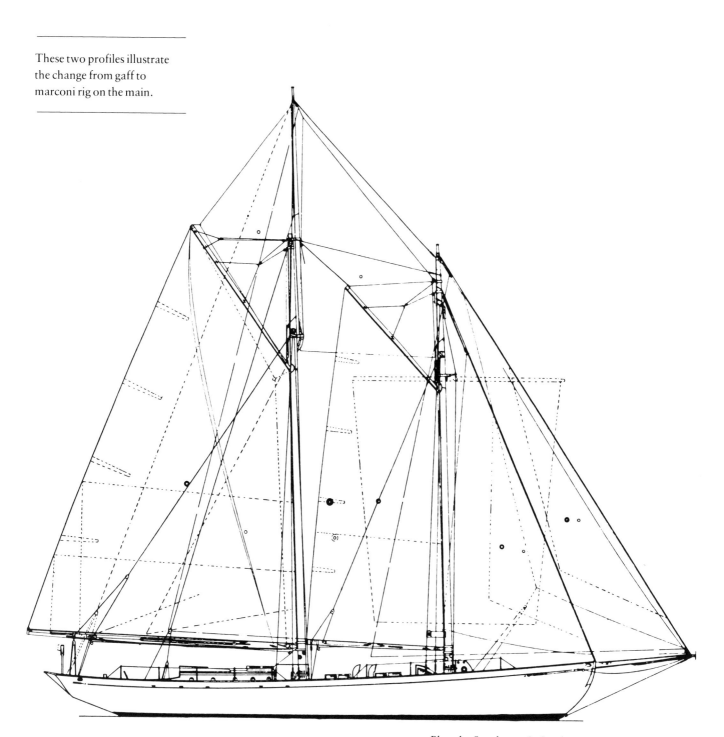

Plans by Sparkman & Stephens

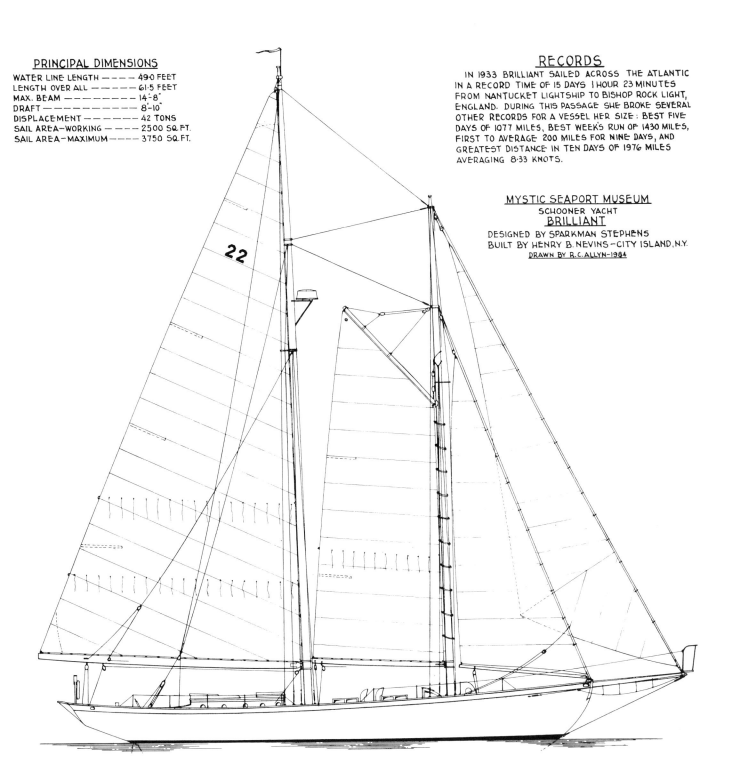

PRINCIPAL DIMENSIONS

WATER LINE LENGTH — — — — 49·0 FEET
LENGTH OVER ALL — — — — — 61·5 FEET
MAX. BEAM — — — — — — — — 14'-8"
DRAFT — — — — — — — — — — 8'-10"
DISPLACEMENT — — — — — — 42 TONS
SAIL AREA—WORKING — — — 2500 SQ.FT.
SAIL AREA—MAXIMUM — — — 3750 SQ.FT.

RECORDS

IN 1933 BRILLIANT SAILED ACROSS THE ATLANTIC
IN A RECORD TIME OF 15 DAYS 1 HOUR 23 MINUTES
FROM NANTUCKET LIGHTSHIP TO BISHOP ROCK LIGHT,
ENGLAND. DURING THIS PASSAGE SHE BROKE SEVERAL
OTHER RECORDS FOR A VESSEL HER SIZE: BEST FIVE
DAYS OF 1077 MILES, BEST WEEK'S RUN OF 1430 MILES,
FIRST TO AVERAGE 200 MILES FOR NINE DAYS, AND
GREATEST DISTANCE IN TEN DAYS OF 1976 MILES
AVERAGING 8·33 KNOTS.

MYSTIC SEAPORT MUSEUM
SCHOONER YACHT
BRILLIANT
DESIGNED BY SPARKMAN STEPHENS
BUILT BY HENRY B. NEVINS — CITY ISLAND, N.Y.
DRAWN BY R.C. ALLYN—1984